Honesty
due dress
Compassion

FUNCTIONAL BUSINESS
PRESENTATIONS

PAUL R. TIMM

Brigham Young University

FUNCTIONAL BUSINESS PRESENTATIONS:

getting across

PRENTICE-HALL, INC., *Englewood Cliffs, New Jersey 07632*

Library of Congress Cataloging in Publication Data

Timm, Paul R
    Functional business presentations.

    Includes bibliographical references and index.
    1. Communication in management. 2. Public
speaking.   I. Title.
HF5718.T54   658.4'5   80-20356
ISBN 0-13-331470-7

Editorial/production supervision and
   interior design by Alice Erdman
Cover design by Jerry Pfeifer
Manufacturing buyer: Gordon Osbourne

Printed in the United States of America
10 9 8 7 6 5

Prentice-Hall International, Inc., *London*
Prentice-Hall of Australia Pty. Limited, *Sydney*
Prentice-Hall of Canada, Ltd., *Toronto*
Prentice-Hall of India Private Limited, *New Delhi*
Prentice-Hall of Japan, Inc., *Tokyo*
Prentice-Hall of Southeast Asia Pte. Ltd., *Singapore*
Whitehall Books Limited, *Wellington, New Zealand*

CONTENTS

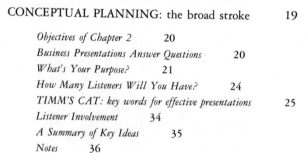

3

ANALYZING YOUR LISTENERS: educated guesses 37

4

PREPARING YOUR MIND 49

5

STATING AND SUPPORTING KEY IDEAS 71

6

ARRANGING IDEAS FOR CLARITY AND IMPACT   83

7

BEGINNINGS, TRANSITIONS, AND ENDINGS: the ties that bind   101

8

ADD A LITTLE LIFE TO YOUR STYLE: holding listener interest   115

9

VISUAL AIDS: sharpen key points, focus the picture   129

10

DELIVERING THE PRESENTATION   151

11

PERSUASIVE MESSAGES: how they work (when they do)   169

12

INSTRUCTIONAL PRESENTATIONS: special considerations   189

PREFACE

This book was written for all people who have been subjected to boring, ill-prepared business presentations—and who don't want to retaliate.

More and more, everyday business calls for the oral presentation of ideas in a concise, well-planned and effective manner. Ineffective presentations sap human energy and waste the time of all concerned. But they do much more than that.

The poorly prepared, carelessly presented oral presentation creates ripples that go far beyond the specific communicative attempt. It creates feelings in its listeners ranging from resentment to hostility or, at best, pity for the inept communicator. But it conveys too, a negative—and potentially costly—image of the organization, cause, enterprise, and character of the speaker. Put bluntly, an ineffective communicator can make himself and all that he represents look pretty dumb.

Yet many leaders who are called upon in their everyday work to convey important ideas orally, have received little or no relevant training. In reality, making a good presentation—whether it is a sales pitch, a briefing, or a public speech—is not difficult. Anyone can learn to do so with a little guidance.

This book aims to offer such guidance, concisely and interestingly, and to give the reader practical, usable information. Whether you use this book as a text in a college course, as an aid in a training program, or as a guide for your personal self-development, you'll find it full of useful ideas. Ideas that will help you in GETTING ACROSS!

THANKS TO . . .

the many people who have helped me to learn about communication over the years in academia, organizations, and at home. Among these are:

- my first speech teachers, Charles R. Petrie, Jr. and Michael H. Prosser who showed me the opportunities in communication
- my graduate school advisors and professors, the late Gordon Wiseman, Carl Weaver, Paul H. Boase, Theodore Clevenger, Jr., and especially Clarence W. Edney who showed me the thrill of accomplishment
- my friend and colleague, Carol McFarland Baxter who coauthored early drafts of several chapters

- the many speakers experienced in seven years of corporate work who bored me to tears, but who provided some great examples for this book
- my parents, wife, and children who taught me love: the most important form of communication.

To them I dedicate this book.

FUNCTIONAL BUSINESS PRESENTATIONS

1

COMMUNICATION:
the manager's critical
competency

OBJECTIVES OF CHAPTER 1

After studying this chapter, the reader should be able to:

1. Explain the interrelationships between communication and management skills.
2. Describe some key roadblocks to understanding which arise from psychological factors and language usage.
3. Identify distinctions between communication efficiency and effectiveness.
4. Identify key characteristics of oral presentations.
5. Describe disadvantages and advantages of the oral presentation as a communication medium.

"As soon as you move one step up from the bottom, your effectiveness depends on your ability to reach others through the spoken or the written word. And the further away your job is from manual work, the larger the organization of which you are an employee, the more important it will be that you know how to convey your thoughts in writing or speaking. In the very large organization . . . this ability to express oneself is perhaps the most important of all the skills a man can possess."[1]

Management scholar Peter F. Drucker made that widely accepted statement almost thirty years ago. His statement isn't "armchair theory." It's an assertion that is widely supported by experience. Numerous surveys of business people in all areas show that there is a profound need for communication skills. One such study polled 3,800 engineering graduates who had entered the profession over a 45-year period. When asked to rank a list of items most important to their general education, they identified as primary, the ability "to express one's thoughts effectively."[2] In a survey of 13,386 college graduates working for General Electric Company, communication skills were cited as of extreme value in business success. Even the engineers in that survey listed communication second only to mathematics in importance to them on the job.[3]

Effective communication helps organizations get things done right. Ineffective communication costs organizations and people hours and dollars. The effect is clear, though not always clearly quantifiable. Poor communication will sap personal and organizational energy and resources.

Despite this, many people who manage the efforts of others have had little training in this crucially important skill. In most college programs, future managers are exposed to little more than a single course in business communication, a subject area that is often synonymous with letter-writing. There is much more to managerial communication than letter-writing.

MANAGEMENT IS COMMUNICATION

Ask a college junior majoring in business administration, "What do managers do?" and you're likely to hear some variation of Henri Fayol's 1916 definition of management functions: planning, organization, commanding, coordinating, and controlling. Ask another student, "What is management?" and she's likely to recite, "The process of getting work accomplished through the efforts of others." If we probe a bit by asking, *"How* does the manager 'coordinate' or 'get work accomplished through others'?" inevitably we'd conclude that managers accomplish their essential work by talking, listening, reading, and writing.

These four activities are orchestrated by the skillful manager to bring about *understanding* and to *influence behaviors* of people working together. Organizations emerge from repeated patterns of communication among members who are (or should be) striving toward similar goals. Clarifying these agreed-upon goals and tasks is a foremost managerial responsibility. Without understanding and influence, there can be no cooperative effort, no organization, no accomplishment of group objectives. Without communication, humanity's accomplishments would be limited to what one individual could do working alone, no more.

Perhaps it would be helpful to consider the term *"communication"* for a moment. The term *"communication"* is widely used in at least three contexts. In one sense it has to do with the mechanics of the process of sending and receiving messages. People "communicate" when they talk together or write to each other. Much of this book will deal with techniques for increasing your probability of "success" in such communicating. I put success in quotes because it's a highly relative term. Indeed, the creation of *absolute* understanding among people seldom occurs. Our uniquely individual perceptions, habits of thought, and experiences make it just about impossible for two people to hold precisely the same understanding of an idea. I'll discuss this in more detail later.

In a second context, *"communication"* is sometimes used as a noun— "your recent communication"—describing an actual message. Most of the time this use refers to written messages.

In a third, and broader sense, *"communication"* refers to the whole process of sharing meanings. It involves complex psychological processes as well as outward behaviors which establish an authentic understanding of feelings, ideas, or values. It is the creation of mutual understanding among two or more parties.

Although this book emphasizes mostly the first use of the term—the process of sending and receiving messages—we cannot ignore implications of the broader meaning of communication as the creation of understanding. This creation of understanding is an exceedingly complex process. The major roadblocks to the achievement of relatively high degrees of understanding arise from the facts that

1.   Our individuality makes *absolute* understanding impossible. As entertainer Mike Nichols once said, "You'll never really know what I mean, and I'll never know exactly what you mean." We are incapable of a perfect empathy. Even "walking a mile in another's shoes" cannot cause us to see the world through the other person's eyes.

2.   The language (words and other symbols) we use to communicate are woefully inadequate to convey complex ideas. As someone said, "Words are pegs to hang ideas on." Words are signs or labels *we* give to *our* ideas. Each of us attaches labels in different and individual ways based on our personal uniqueness. Often people confuse the label with the idea itself, forgetting (or failing to recognize) that the word is not the thing; the peg it hangs on is not the idea it describes. John Locke said, "We should have a great many fewer disputes in the world if words were taken for what they are, the signs of our ideas only, and not for things themselves."

3.   Most of us don't want to be better understanders. It is, perhaps ironic, but I think true, that few people really want to understand others—especially when there is the risk of being exposed to a point of view contrary to our own. The more we seek to understand others, the more their ideas may begin to make sense! And that can be scary! We'd all like to be better communicators so long as that term connotes an ability to persuade, instruct, motivate, or even manipulate. But when communication is seen as the creation of understanding, we are less enthralled with the prospect.

It may be profitable to elaborate on these three underlying conditions which lead to communication barriers. I said a few moments ago that our individuality makes it difficult, if not impossible, to *absolutely* understand others; to absolutely communicate. This deserves clarification.

INDIVIDUAL DIFFERENCES COMPLICATE COMMUNICATION

Each of us, from the very beginning of our lives, has had unique and individual experiences. Scientists tell us that every sensory experience—that is, everything we have ever felt, tasted, heard, seen and so forth—is recorded in the memory banks of our brain. From the very beginning of our lives, we experience things that no other person has experienced in exactly the same way. Each new sensory message received is interpreted in terms of things that we have experienced in the past. The past events color and shade our interpretation of present events.

To make sense of all these experiences, we attach labels or words to describe them both to ourselves and to others. Your stock of usable words limits your ability to share these experiences with others. These word labels are likely to carry certain connotations, either positive, negative, or neutral. Let me give you a simple example. Suppose that as a very small child you were mauled by a large dog. It seems very likely that the word "dog" will have a negative connotation, even arouse a distinct fear response in you. On the other hand, if you have had very pleasant experiences with dogs as a child, the term is likely to arouse a very pleasant association. More to the point, we may associate pleasant recollections of the term "Christmas Season" as we think of the holiday festivities, while retail sales clerks may dread the hustle and bustle of crowded stores and impatient customers. A favorable experience with minority race employees may make a manager enthusiastic about "affirmative action programs," while the same term could cause a personnel manager to shudder.

People not only do not see the world in the same way because of their different experiences and perceptions, but in a fairly literal sense, people don't even *live in* the same psychological world. Each new message we receive is evaluated in terms of what we already "know" to determine if it makes sense. What makes perfectly good sense for me, may be utter nonsense for you. In many cases, of course, the magnitude of our different understandings about terms may not be significant. But my point is that it is highly unlikely that we will give *exactly* the same meaning to any particular event.

LANGUAGE COMPLICATES COMMUNICATION

The second roadblock to understanding is that language can seldom adequately convey complex ideas. Language plays a key role in communication in at least two areas. First, we assign language terms or symbols to our sensory experiences to give them a name. We then use this label internally—as we perceive and think—in the development of our personal sense of reality. These labels are also used when we attempt to share our experiences with other individuals. It has been estimated that we, in the English language, have approximately 600,000 standard words available for use. We might add to that several hundred thousand additional technical terms, acronyms, jargon or slang expressions giving us a total potential vocabulary of somewhere near a million words. Interestingly, however, the average adult seems to use only about 2,000 words on a regular basis. The dilemma arises, of course, when we consider the meager store of accepted symbols which are used to communicate an infinite number of different ideas.

The dilemma of language is further compounded when we consider that much of what we communicate to others is in the form of *nonverbal* "languages." Some experts suggest that as much as 70 or 80 percent of the *meaning* received comes from nonverbal cues. Such things as our personal appearance and dress, our facial expression, gestures, use of time and space, and many other factors contribute to or detract from the establishment of clear understanding.

We get distracted by the *way* people talk and miss the intent of their messages. We allow ourselves to get turned off (or turned on) by the language and fail to objectively or rationally process the intended meaning. All of this gives support to what psychologist William James said: "The most immutable barrier in nature is between one man's thoughts and another's."

MANY PEOPLE DON'T WANT TO BE BETTER COMMUNICATORS

The final roadblock to understanding I mentioned is that most of us don't want to be better understanders. It's ironic that most of us would say that we really want to be better communicators, yet we seldom want to make the effort to understand more clearly the receivers of our messages. To get out of ourselves and into another person's thought patterns involves changes in our own behavior. Our behaviors, including ways we attempt to communicate, are expressions of our personality, the total of our psychological makeup. We have a vested interest in the ways we've been thinking and acting. We are usually much more willing and comfortable getting *other people* to change the way *they* do things than in getting ourselves to change our way of thinking and acting. To be a better communicator requires mental flexibility and effort. And most of all, it requires sincere desire to understand others so that we can help them understand us. When we get to the point where we spend as much time and effort in diagnosing and analyzing our audiences as we do in preparing the actual messages we have to give them, we are well on our way to becoming better communicators. I'll talk more about this in Chapter 3.

Communication is the establishment of understanding and the effective use of influence. To be successful we need to recognize that this is at least a two-way street. A communicator cannot, by himself, successfully communicate. It is the message receiver who will determine whether or not the communicator is successful.

The manager who recognizes this dependence on listeners or readers for communication success will be light years ahead of the "I-oriented" talker.

KINDS OF COMMUNICATION SKILLS
USED BY MANAGERS

The four basic communication skills—reading, writing, speaking, and listening—are each important to the manager. One measure of relative importance may be, however, the amount of time spent in each. One study by Jeffrey Auer[4] concluded that oral skills (e.g., talking and listening) were used three times as often as reading and writing skills. According to Auer, administrators spend their communication time on the job this way:

- 16% reading
- 9% writing
- 45% listening
- 30% speaking

Henry Mintzberg's extensive studies of managerial work concluded that there is a strong attraction to verbal media among managers.*

"Virtually every empirical study of managerial time allocation draws attention to the great proportion of time spent in verbal communication, with estimates ranging from 57 percent of time . . . by foreman . . . to 89 percent of episodes in verbal interaction by middle managers in a manufacturing company . . . [one study] found that conversation comsumed 80 percent of the middle managers' time. My own findings bear this out . . . verbal interaction accounted for 78 percent of the five managers' time and 67 percent of their activities."[5]

In a recent survey, Harold T. Smith polled a group of skilled and effective managers to determine what abilities or competencies they considered to be crucial to their jobs. Seven of the eleven skills designated as "super critical" or "highly critical" for managerial success involved oral communication as shown in the table on page 8.[6]

This emphasis on oral communication should not, of course, be construed as depreciating the importance of writing skills. There is abundant evidence that writing effectiveness is essential to managerial success. In this book, however, I address that critical competency which often appears as an afterthought in other books in business communication: the oral presentation of ideas in the business environment. My contention is that business com-

*Mintzberg uses the term "verbal" to mean *oral* as opposed to written. Other writers, myself included, reserve the term "verbal" to refer to the use of *words* as opposed, for example, to nonverbal graphics, gestures, body language, vocal tone, appearance, and so forth.

20 CRITICAL MANAGERIAL COMPETENCIES

Importance Rating		*Survey Rank & Competency*
Super Critical	1	Listen actively
	2	Give clear, effective instructions
	3	Accept your share of responsibility for problems
	4	Identify real problem
Highly Critical	5	Manage time; set priorities
	6	Give recognition for excellent performance
	7	Communicate decisions to employees
	8	Communicate effectively (orally)
	9	Shift priorities if necessary
	10	Explain work
	11	Obtain and provide feedback in two-way communication sessions
Critical	12	Write effectively
	13	Prepare action plan
	14	Define job qualifications
	15	Effectively implement organizational change
	16	Explain and use cost reduction methods
	17	Prepare and operate within a budget
	18	Develop written goals
	19	Justify new personnel and capital equipment
	20	Participate in seminars and read

munication is more than letters, memos and written reports. Managers (or students training for management) would be wise to polish oral communication skills too. In short, we need training in getting across to others via the spoken word.

COMMUNICATORS: CHOOSE YOUR MEDIA!

An ongoing concern of the effective manager is, "How can we best get the information needed to the people who will use it?" The impact on the receiver of a written memo, a formal letter, a group presentation, or a personal interview will be very different. So which works best?

To select appropriate media, we should recognize a distinction between communication *efficiency* and *effectiveness*. Efficiency is a simple ratio between the resources, such as time, materials, and effort, expended in generating messages and the number of people to whom the message is sent. To improve efficiency, we simply increase the number of people reached or reduce the message preparation cost in some way. The widely distributed memo or mass meeting is an efficient communication method.

Communication *effectiveness* is something else, however. In organizations, effective communication is that which creates understanding and which influences people toward the accomplishment of group goals. Saul Gellerman, the management theorist, concludes that organizational communication ". . . may be said to be 'effective' when a message is:

- *received* by its intended audience,
- *interpreted* in essentially the same way by the recipients as by the senders,
- *remembered* for reasonable extended periods of time, and
- *used* when appropriate occasions arise."[7]

The dilemma for the manger is that, in most cases, the communications methods that are most efficient are least effective, and vice versa. In almost every case, face-to-face oral presentations to an individual or a small group of people is the least efficient, least convenient, and most costly method of communication. It is also the most *effective.*

Gellerman concludes that an unwillingness to pay the price for effectiveness in communication may well be false economy. "A very large part of the blame for ineffective communication . . . falls on management's persistent efforts to communicate with the most people at the least cost. Alas, communication is one function where it does not pay to be efficient."[8]

THE VALUE OF ORAL PRESENTATIONS

An oral presentation to an individual or to a small group of people can be an extremely effective way of conveying important information and asserting influence. Some of the most important advantages of using this communication medium are that it is capable of conveying rather complex information in a structured, logical arrangement in a manner that provides direct and immediate feedback. The feedback lets you know if you are succeeding.

If your talk seems to bring on that dreaded audience virus, the symptoms of which are yawns, throat-clearing, murmuring among listeners, and the catatonic stare of the "wide-asleep listener," something is wrong. Either the topic is not worth the cost of delivery, or you are failing to get the audience involved. The immediate feedback gives you an opportunity to regroup and try again. A letter or written report would not provide a second chance.

If your audience appears confused or disturbed, as indicated by facial expression, restlessness, questioning among themselves, you can and must adjust your message to clarify or at least seek to understand what's confusing them. You can't do this in a letter or memo.

In most business presentation situations there are opportunities for even more than nonverbal feedback. Listeners have an opportunity to ask questions, to raise issues, to make suggestions of their own. In fact, as you'll see later in this book, the effective communicator will provide opportunities for listener involvement in what is being said. By gaining the involvement of our listeners, we gain higher degrees of commitment to the issues or topics being presented as well as better understanding. *Communication is participation in a joint effort to understand.*

Is the immediate feedback available in oral presentations valuable enough to offset the expenditure of time, extra effort, and possible speaker anxiety? The answer is an unequivocal—sometimes. Key considerations include: (1) How important is it that we get a high degree of understanding? (2) How complex is the message? (3) Is it important to retain a "hard copy" of the message for future reference or as proof that the message was conveyed? (4) What is the feasibility (and cost) of getting together in person? and (5) How good are the oral communication skills of the presenter as compared to his or her writing skills?

While a carefully prepared oral presentation is not cheap, neither is the written media. A variety of costs should be considered when making media comparisons.

In organizational communication, your highest media expenditures are usually people costs: the wages and benefits paid to employees. There are, however, also technical costs. These include the price of paper, postage, photocopying, typewriters, telephones, videotape players, and so forth. A simple face-to-face conversation between two executives may involve no technical costs whatsoever but considerable people costs. Written media costs also include subtle dimensions which are often not considered. For example, an accurate cost picture should include expenditures for operating the mail room, filing cabinets, in and out baskets for distribution of messages, and even the square footage of valuable office space occupied by these artifacts of the written communication system as well as the cost of disposing of waste paper. When all such figures are considered and added to the people costs, written communication can amount to anywhere between a penny and ten cents a word.

Even the best written communications, however, do not allow for immediate feedback from message receivers. Therein lies the most significant drawback to the written medium. In situations where it is important to get responses, indications of agreement, disagreement, or assurances that the information is being received and understood, the oral communication media make more sense. While it is not always economically feasible to present information to people on an individual basis, the oral presentation in the business context can be adapted to audiences of many sizes. Although it may be, for example, very expensive to meet with each employee to explain a

relatively simple new procedure, say, the use of a new company f
group could be instructed in an economical and yet effective man.
carefully prepared oral presentation. In addition, testing for understanding
this material could be carried out on the spot to see that the message has been
received.

PRESENTATIONS: A SPECIAL FORM OF ORAL COMMUNICATION

There are, of course, many forms of oral communication used in businesses.
Informal face-to-face conversation, telephone discussions, employee interviews, and group problem-solving sessions each call for oral skills and varying
degrees of preparation.

The oral presentation is more formal than other kinds of oral communication. It is used when your information is more complex or more important
than matters discussed in routine conversation. It calls for *careful planning and
organizing*. Often, though not always, the audience will be larger than the
audience for routine or informal oral messages. But the key characteristics of
the business presentation are that it is

- purposeful
- planned
- organized

The *purposes* of oral presentations may vary widely. Here are some
situations with clearly different purposes:

1. You must bring new policy information before a group of department
   heads in their staff meeting.
2. You must justify a budget you have prepared for your office or department
   before an executive committe.
3. You are asked to "say a few words" at a retirement dinner for your boss.
4. You call on a potential customer or client to discuss your product or
   service and sell him on it.
5. You must convince a special interest group that your company is aware of
   its concerns.
6. You are asked to speak at meetings of your business or professional
   association.

In these cases, sending a memo or letter won't do. And going before a
group for an informal chat—without plan or organization of ideas—could be
disastrous. It's a time for getting across with an effective oral presentation.

PRESENTATIONS: SOME DISADVANTAGES

There are, of course, disadvantages to presentational speaking. When compared to written media, it has several drawbacks.

First, your audience cannot later review or study your presentation as they could if the information were in writing. (We will, however, explore ways for compensating for that disadvantage later in this book.)

Second, the spoken word, once delivered, is difficult to retract. You can more easily put your foot in your mouth. Written communication, on the other hand, can be revised, analyzed, and corrected many times before the audience sees the final results. This problem makes us doubly aware of the need to plan presentations well and to deliver them carefully.

Third, the oral presentation may be given at a time that is not most conducive to success. A well-prepared talk can fall flat because of timing factors beyond the control of the speaker. Your listeners may be distracted by a recent disagreement or some distracting news which arrived shortly before your scheduled presentation. A written report can, of course, be set aside until the reader is in a more receptive frame of mind. The oral presentation must be attended to now.

PRESENTATIONS: THE BIG ADVANTAGE IS YOU!

But the oral presentation has one distinct advantage: YOU! *You have personal powers* for conveying messages that the best bond paper and the best press or typist can never duplicate:

- Your voice offers numerous possibilities for variety and emphasis.

- Your gestures, facial expressions, and body movement can convey enthusiasm and interest that is contagious.

- Your personality and appearance can generate trust and allay suspicions or doubts.

- Your sensitivity to listener feedback and adjustment to their information needs can ensure a high degree of understanding.

These personal powers aren't natural traits some people have and others don't. They arise from sensitivity and skills which anyone can develop. The payoff for developing such communicative power is enormous. Through training in effective presentations, people will (1) like you or at least respect you when you speak, (2) cooperate with you, (3) understand what you say, and (4) believe you when you say it.

BUSINESS PRESENTATIONS AND
PUBLIC SPEAKING:
WHAT ARE THE DIFFERENCES?

One executive recently responded to a question about the adequacy of communication training in business schools this way: "Students are being taught oral skills in school, but not the ones they need in a business environment. They are prepared to make speeches but not to present reports, discuss statistics, or conduct a business meeting."[9]

One motive for writing this book is that I have been unable to locate a text that takes into account the important differences between public speaking and business presentations. Although I readily admit that we can learn much from a course in public speaking, and that many principles of public speech preparation can apply to business presentations, there remain important differences.

First, presentational speaking in organizations can often be categorized as "private" speaking. That is, it takes place "within the family," among people who know each other and who share common organizational language and understanding. Presumably, they also share common goals—those relating to the advancement of the organization. Listener analysis, a crucial factor in speaking effectiveness, can be enhanced by simply going to those with whom you will speak and gathering data about their specific wants and needs. This is seldom possible in public speech situations.

Secondly, the ongoing effects of presentations are more apparent in business organizations. For the public speaker who "bombs," the worst that can occur is that his listeners won't be too excited about hearing him again. Or they won't vote for her. Or they will simply be disappointed that the talk wasn't better. But the business manager must continue to interact with that audience. The loss of listener confidence resulting from a poor presentation can carry over to other interactions among these people. On the positive side, of course, a manager who gets a reputation for giving effective presentations may benefit from a "halo" effect that carries over to other job activities. In many respects, we have more to lose by flopping in a business presentation and more to gain by succeeding, than the typical public speaker. At least so far as our organizational reputation—and our career growth—is concerned.

A third difference between business presentations and most public speaking is in the choice of topic. Many basic speech texts spend several pages teaching students how to select a topic for speeches. In business, we often find the topics thrust upon us by organizational needs.

A fourth difference is in the size of our audiences. The public speaker gears her presentation to what some authors call the "one-to-many" speech situation. Frequently, speeches must be tailored to the mass audience and interaction with them is severely limited. On the other hand, most business

Human Behavior Magazine

*"Before we adjourn I have a personal word
for each of you.
Foster: Seize the initiative
Blakeleigh: Watch the competition
Leventhal: Hang Tough
Hutchinson: Cut the costs
Kalmus: Hit the road"*

Business presentations often permit more personalized messages than public speaking

Source: From *Good News, Bad News* by Henry Martin. Copyright © 1969, 1970, 1971, 1972, 1973, 1974, 1975, 1976, 1977 Henry R. Martin. Used by permission of Charles Scribner's Sons.

presentations are made to individuals or small groups. Direct reactions from listeners—even to the extent of answering and clarifying questions as the talk is presented—are readily available. The business audience is more involved; there is more exchange with the speaker. Remember, the defining characteristics of the oral presentation situation—purpose, planning and organization— say nothing about audience size. An audience of one or two listeners is not uncommon.

SUCCESSFUL COMMUNICATORS GET AHEAD!

No single skill relates to management or leadership success more strongly than the ability to communicate effectively. The active exchange of information and ideas is the lifeblood of any organization. And successful business executives recognize this.

Communication is what managers *do*. While writing and reading are important, the spoken word is most often used to establish understanding and provide direction which influences organizational outcomes. The ability to present information clearly is a valuable personal asset. To illustrate that companies recognize the value of this skill, we need only look at what they are spending to cultivate it.

Recently, consulting firms specializing in teaching presentational speaking have sprung up in major cities across the country. One New York company charges business people $900 for an intensive two-day course. Asked why companies would spend money in such a way, one "graduate" of the course vigorously defended its practical value: "So many business decisions are challenged these days by government officials and special interest groups that the ability to speak out effectively in defense of corporate activities has become critically important for top executives."[10]

But there are other applications besides "defending corporate activities" that you as a practicing manager will be called upon to use. And you don't have to wait to become a top executive to begin using such skills. Every person in a managerial position—that is, one who works with and through other individuals and groups to accomplish organizational goals—needs skill in oral presentations. Other factors being equal, a speaker who is effective will advance faster in his career than one who is not. The ability to present informtion in an orderly, interesting and understandable manner is at the heart of the managerial process.

Now, having said all that about the importance and value of speaking skills, I'd like to say also . . .

THIS BOOK WILL DO YOU NO GOOD

. . . unless you are willing to do more than just read it. The objective is to provide you with some key ideas, presented in a concise format, which will show you how to prepare better for getting across to others in presentations.

As you work with this book, *apply* some of the suggestions offered to change the way you *do* things, not just change the ways you think. There is a difference between learning *about* communication and improving your actual communication skills. This book is based on behavioral assumptions: knowledge is of value to the extent that it affects the ways the reader *does* something with it. Vincent DiSalvo suggests that we adjust our expectations to meet those of the behavioral science perspective to get the maximum value from communication training. Based on an article by Culbert and Schmidt, DiSalvo[11] compares traditional and behavioral expectations (see p. 16.)

Make it your objective to go beyond learning *about* presentational speaking. Use this book as a springboard for active, creative thought and application.

Too often when we consider human communication, we eagerly identify

Traditional Expectations	Behavioral Science Expectations
1. Improving my competence in communicating is like learning about anything else. If I learn the guiding principles which apply, I shall be a better communicator.	1. Knowledge is not behavior. Improving one's effectiveness in communicating involves much more than learning new terms and concepts.
2. There is an objective body of knowledge—a set of rules which work regardless of the person applying them.	2. In improving one's communication, the person must first recognize his own style of behavior and attitudes, beliefs, and the personal assumptions underlying them.
3. The learner's responsibility is to listen to the conceptualizations of the expert. In that way the learner will become more expert himself and *later* will be able to apply the learnings.	3. Personal experience and analysis must *precede* conceptualization of learnings. Therefore, the learner must *first* become an *active participant.*

problems others have, but fail to take a hard critical look at our own. If you're sincere about improving communication skills, you'll be willing to make changes in the way *you* have been doing things.

To maximize your benefits from this book, I'd like to suggest a few ideas:

1. As you read, try to tie the information in with experiences or ideas that you are reminded of. The book has ample margins so that as you read you can "talk back" to me by penciling in your thoughts. Get in the habit of doing that regularly. As you work on the book, the book will work on you.

2. Go back to the learning objectives after studying each chapter. They are designed to stimulate thought and help you focus on the key ideas presented. Use them to test yourself.

3. Most important of all, be willing to try on new behaviors that may at first seem awkward or uncomfortable. You may be pleasantly surprised at the responses you get from others—and the feelings of success you get inside.

4. Participate in the free and honest critique of your fellow students. And be *appreciative* of the feedback they give you. Even if you don't fully agree (or don't agree at all!), their insights will be useful in indicating how others see you. (If you are not using this book in a classroom or group training program, seek out trusted associates—people whose advice you value—and *ask for* feedback about your communication skills. Be careful to ask in ways that will get you specific information.)

5. Keep an open mind. Some of the ideas presented here may not work in every situation. Communicating is an art, not a science. But if your mind is prematurely closed, you'll pass up real opportunities to develop communication skills. Remember a closed mind is like a closed fist: You can neither give nor receive with it—all you can do is knock things down.

6. Finally, remember that all effective communicators are truly self-made. All that a guide can do is point out some of the techniques known to have been

effective in the past. From there on, it's up to you to develop your personal power.

Good luck on your personal journey toward greater communication, skill, and a better, more successful you.

CHAPTER 1. A SUMMARY OF KEY IDEAS

1. Management *is* communication. Managers accomplish their essential work through communication.
2. Human communication is an exceedingly complex process which involves the total psychology of participants and which is subject to myriad complicating effects. Barriers and breakdowns should be expected. Perfection in creating absolute understanding should not be expected.
3. Major roadblocks to the creation of understanding arise from our individual natures, our language use, and our desire to communicate effectively.
4. Managers use speaking and listening more heavily than writing and reading.
5. Communication *efficiency* (the ratio between resources expanded and number of people reached) is different from and may be inversely related to communication *effectiveness*. Managers often forfeit effectiveness in search of efficiency.
6. Effective oral presentations provide occasions for participation in a joint effort to create understanding.
7. A business presentation is a form of oral communication that is *purposeful, planned,* and *organized*.
8. Disadvantages of oral presentations include a lack of a hard copy for later study, the difficulty of retracting unintended slips, and possible distractions created by timing or environment surrounding the talk.
9. A major advantage of the oral presentation is the opportunity to convey enthusiasm and project an appropriate image that may not come across in a written medium.
10. Business presentations tend to differ from public speaking situations in that
    (a) the audience is usually better known and probably shares common goals
    (b) the speaker's organizational reputation is subject to positive or negative evaluations which may well influence future work

      (c) the topic of a talk is usually dictated by organizational need rather than personal whim

      (d) audiences tend to be smaller, permitting more listener involvement

11.   No single skill relates to management or leadership success more strongly than the ability to communicate effectively.

NOTES

1.   Peter F. Drucker. *People and Performance: The Best of Peter Drucker on Management* (New York: Harpers College Press, 1977), pp. 262–263.

2.   Dean S. Ellis. *Management and Administrative Communication* (New York: Macmillan, 1978), p. 359.

3.   Ibid.

4.   J. Jeffery Auer. *An Introduction to Research in Speech* (New York: Harper & Row, Pub., 1959).

5.   Henry Mintzberg. *The Nature of Managerial Work* (New York: Harper & Row, Pub., 1973), p. 38.

6.   Harold T. Smith. "20 Critical Competencies for Managers," *Management World,* January 1978.

7.   Saul W. Gellerman. *The Management of Human Resources* (Hinsdale, Ill.: Dryden Press, 1976), p. 61.

8.   Ibid, p. 62.

9.   Homer L. Cox. "If at First You Don't Succeed, Try Another Tack," *The ABCA Bulletin,* Vol. 42, No. 2, June 1979, pp. 1–6.

10.   "A $900 Lesson in Podium Power," *Fortune,* August 1977, p. 196.

11.   Vincent DiSalvo. *Business and Professional Communication* (Columbus: Charles E. Merrill, 1977), p. 8.

2

CONCEPTUAL PLANNING:
the broad strokes

OBJECTIVES OF CHAPTER 2

After studying this chapter, the reader should be able to

1. Specify the nature of the questions answered by a given presentation.
2. Explain the importance of clarifying the purpose of a presentation before further planning begins.
3. Identify the different emphases of persuasive, instructional or progress report presentations.
4. Explain how audience size and specific target listeners must be considered in planning the talk.
5. Name the elements of conceptual planning identified by the acronym, TIMMS CAT and give examples of each.
6. Describe techniques for increasing listener involvement and participation in a business presentation.

The old caution to "engage brain before putting mouth in motion" is good advice. Getting ideas across calls for clarity of purpose, careful planning and creative organization of thoughts. And this needs to be done before we start to talk. As William Penn said, "If thou thinkest twice, before thou speakest once, thou wilt speak twice the better for it."

In this chapter, I will survey some of the general characteristics of oral presentations and suggest a series of elements that should be brought into your planning very early in the process. Some ways to apply this conceptual framework will also be provided. This material should be considered before developing the specifics of your message.

BUSINESS PRESENTATIONS ANSWER QUESTIONS

Oral presentations and briefings provide the organization with digestable *information*. Information is the oxygen of a working organization; it reduces uncertainty, clarifies scope, purpose and direction for people in the system. Your approach to presenting ideas is determined by the underlying questions—the needs for clarification—faced by the organization or its members. Sometimes the real questions are not clearly asked, let alone answered. The executive who asked a staff attorney for a "clarification" on changes in

"Bradley, are you visualizing, synthesizing, conceptualizing, analyzing, finalizing, or catching up on your sleep?"

Conceptual planning means thinking through the whole communication process before developing the specific message

government safety regulations may really have been asking, How can we get around the law? The progress report requested by a prime contractor from a subcontractor may seek answers to questions about the feasibility of using the company on future contracts as well as how are you doing on the current job.

Before we prepare an oral presentation, we would do well to list as many possible questions as we can. And don't just ask the obvious ones; dig a little to anticipate what else might be on the mind of your listeners. A talk that fails to address relevant listener concerns falls flat. Having all the answers, but to the wrong questions, doesn't help.

WHAT'S YOUR PURPOSE

The ancient philosopher Seneca said, "Our plans miscarry because they have no aim. When a man does not know what harbor he is making for, no wind is the right wind." If you don't know where you are going with an oral presentation, you'll never know whether or not you've succeeded. On the positive side, there is great power in focusing your mental energy on clearly-defined goals. This must be a first step in planning an oral presentation.

After you have anticipated your audience's concerns and questions, turn inward and ask yourself some questions. What exactly do you hope to accomplish? How will your listeners respond after you finish? What results will you attain? What specific actions would you like to see from your listeners? Answers to these questions define your purpose and provide criteria against which you can measure your degree of success.

The purposes of presentations may be classified into three groups, although overlapping and multiple-purposes are not uncommon. The three classes are presentations to (1) persuade, (2) instruct or explain, and (3) report progress. Let's look at each. A *persuasive presentation* requires you to do three things: convince your listeners of your point of view, get them to agree with that point of view, and get them to *act* on what they have agreed to. The last requirement is especially important because the success of your presentation can be measured by the amount of such action that takes place as a result of your presentation. Persuasion calls for *action.*

Many, perhaps most, business presentations are heavily persuasive. Here are some examples:

1. You must convince your boss that you need an additional $15,000 in your operating budget for the coming fiscal year.
2. You are asked to justify your request for two additional photocopiers for your department.
3. You want to convince your boss that, based on your interviews with several candidates for an internship program, one is clearly superior to the others and should be selected.
4. You want to point out that a recent policy decision regarding disposing of waste products from your manufacturing plant runs a potential risk of being in conflict with Environmental Protection Agency regulations, and recommend an alternative plan.

All presentations have some persuasive elements. Anytime we give a talk, we want some action from our listeners although the "action" may be only a mental change of increased understanding. Persuasive situations, however, also assume there is some degree of resistance to your proposals, which is less likely to be present in instructional, explanatory, or report presentations. We attempt to get someone to do something they probably would not normally do without some encouragement.

The second class of presentations is the informative talk. This class can be further broken down into *instructional* or *explanatory* presentations. Instructional presentations offer specific procedures for doing something, while explanatory talks provide your listeners with an opportunity to gain some new knowledge or understanding of a more general nature. The distinction between these is rather subtle but should be kept in mind when defining a specific purpose. Both involve information-giving as their key function. Instruction implies a more "nuts and bolts" orientation, while explanation goes a bit more into the philosophy or background of a policy, procedure, or proposal.

Examples of *instructional* presentations include situations where

1. You "show and tell" a new employee in the Personnel Department how to operate the company's videotape equipment.
2. You teach your department managers how to fill out a new report form designed by the corporate office.
3. You describe the organization's style manual for written documents to a group of new technical writers indicating how they are to use it.

Instructional communication situations invite "testing" your audience for knowledge gained, either through an oral question-answer session, via a written quiz, or by asking your listeners to perform what they have learned to do. Your objective is some degree of skill development.

Explanatory presentations usually give a *general* overall picture of a concept, program, or thing rather than specific techniques of doing something. Your objective is listener understanding.

Explanatory talks may be called for when

1. You orient new employees to company goals, policies, and traditions.
2. You explain the financial considerations which resulted in a major change in the company's sales strategy.
3. You explain the roles to be assumed at a new branch bank to which three employees will be transferred.
4. You forecast the effects on company operations likely to result from recent fuel shortages.

Progress reports are presented to keep your listeners posted on the various stages of a long-term project or goal they are already aware of. Often, progress reports are presented at regular intervals, such as monthly or quarterly, until the project is completed. Examples of progress report situations are:

1. You report on the stages in the development of a new product that your research division is creating.
2. You report on expenditures to date in your department compared to your total yearly budget.
3. You report on your plant's success in reaching production objectives for a specific period.

4.   You report on ongoing efforts to contribute to state or federal programs for energy conservation, environmental improvement, or social awareness programs.

Identifying the type of speaking situation very early in the planning stage should help you to keep on track and more effectively to clarify your purpose and your idea organization strategy.

HOW MANY LISTENERS WILL YOU HAVE?

The number of listeners can vary greatly for business presentations. Sometimes a presentation is designed for only *one individual*. For example, you may explain to your boss a proposed budget you have worked up, or you may present a sales presentation to a purchasing agent who you hope will become a customer. Although often the audience of one is more of an interview (give-and-take) style, the principles of planning and organization of ideas is every bit as important here. Many crucial organizational decisions are made when one or two key people huddle around an effective presentation. Careful planning is especially important when detailed material must be presented in a logical order so that your listener can follow the reasoning clearly. Often, of course, a question-and-answer session will follow your planned message to provide additional clarification.

Another common communication situation in business involves an individual speaking to a *small group* of listeners. An explanation to your bank tellers of how to work with a new form designed by the main branch, or a discussion with the owners of a small company on how they can afford to purchase their own computer are examples of such a case.

Still other occasions require communication with *large groups* of people. For example, you may explain a new retirement program to all salaried employees in your company, or you may give a brief report at the annual stockholder's meeting.

The fewer listeners you address, the greater the opportunities for tailoring your remarks to their individual motives and needs. The trade-off, of course, is that presentations to individuals are more expensive than to larger groups. The efficiency is lower: fewer listeners are reached per each unit of effort.

Your purpose often determines your audience. If you need approval on a decision that can be granted by a single individual working alone, a presentation to that person alone makes sense. If a group response or popular approval is helpful to your purpose, a larger audience should be addressed. Sometimes, however, speakers lose sight of whom they are talking to (i.e., whose decisions really counts). The presence of extra listeners may cloud the fact that one person will make the decision to take the action you seek. For example, the business presentation advocating pay increases for employees may be widely acclaimed by those potentially affected, but fail to convince the individual who must determine the allocation of resources.

Recognizing the real target-listener(s) and keeping the audience as small as practicable permits a focused approach: a rifle instead of a shotgun. It also permits more extensive use of listener involvement techniques which I'll discuss later in this chapter.

In this section, we've been talking only about the *size* of your audience. Consideration of the *nature of your listeners* will be discussed at length in Chapter 3.

TIMM'S CAT: KEY WORDS FOR EFFECTIVE PRESENTATIONS

I find memory aids useful when I am trying to recall a list of key ingredients or components. Here's one I worked up to remember key letters which refer to the ingredients of an effective presentation: TIMM'S CAT.[1] Here's what the letters stand for:

T	*Topic*	Determine specifically what your presentation is about; give it a label or a working title to help identify the message.
I	*Intent*	Determine specifically what you want the audience to learn, think, do, or feel. Why is the presentation to be given? What questions does it answer? Does it get to the heart of the issue or problem?
M	*Materials*	Decide what references, notes, props, visual aids, handouts, films, charts, and equipment will be needed or helpful to achieve your intended results. What will you need to get across to your listeners?
M	*Message*	Determine specifically what you are going to say to your audience, the content of your ideas or report. This will include at least three main parts: (1) *introduction/attention-getter;* (2) *body*—the "pitch" consisting of main points and supporting information aimed at getting some desired response from your listeners; and (3) a *conclusion/action step*.
S	*Summaries*	Restate the main points for your listeners. Tie those points together in some easy-to-remember format. Summaries are not only intended for the end of the talk. Points should be grouped into small bundles and summarized as they are discussed in the presentation.

C	*Check-up*	Test or otherwise check for understanding and retention of the message. Did the listeners get the message? Was your intent fulfilled?
A	*Assignment*	Give the audience something specific to do or think about in the days to come.
T	*Take-home*	Use handouts, samples, reading lists; something for audiences to take with them that can go on reinforcing your message.

That's a quick run through. Now let's elaborate on each element of this functional feline.

Topic

In most situations the topic, in general form, arises from some felt need, unanswered questions, or a particular assignment given to you.

You can clarify your topic by giving it a working title, a statement of your theme. This title should be specific yet need not sound like a newspaper headline. Indeed, a longer, more descriptive title is often better. Instead of talking about "plant safety" we might deal with "reducing accidents in the welding shop." "Billing order accuracy" might become "reducing errors created by key punch operators." Start from a general problem or topic area and narrow it to a specific statement or title for your talk. Also, try to put into your title something to indicate the importance of the topic to your audience. Usually a verb such as "improving" and "reducing," as in the preceding examples, will do this by suggesting that the talk will be beneficial to your listeners. The sooner you can show a listener some benefit to him, the better you'll hold his attention. As Benjamin Disraeli said, "Talk to a man about himself and he will listen for hours."

One way to clarify our topic is to come down the ladder of abstraction from the rather vague to the more concrete. Two terms that are commonly used by semanticists are *extensional meaning* and *intentional meaning*. Extensional meanings are those terms we can experience directly. The word automobile is an extensional word in that we could point to an automobile and say this is what I'm talking about. An extensional term points at the thing it refers to. The meaning of the word automobile is complete by merely pointing or by denoting this object in the real world.

Intentional meanings have no such clear referent. These meanings must be suggested in someone else's mind. The kinds of things described by intentional terms are not tangible, concrete items. A word such as "mobility," "spirit," or "creativity" has intentional meaning and must be further described by other words in order to be made clear.

The more frequently we can use extensional meanings to describe what we're trying to accomplish, the more effective we're likely to be. Let's look at an example frequently heard in businesses. Managers become concerned about employee *morale*. Morale is an intentional term (we can't point to it) which conjures up wildly different meanings in different people. Extensional terms we might more profitably deal with are "absenteeism," "tardiness," "turnover," or "incidents of plant destruction." These can be clearly identified by pointing to examples. Try using extensional terms as you clarify the theme of your talk.

In many situations, of course, your title will never be known to your listeners; we seldom announce it except in more formal public speaking situations. The title does, however, serve to (1) specify and limit the scope of your topic, (2) remind you to relate what you will say to listener benefits, (3) identify your topic on the agenda of a meeting (where appropriate), and (4) provide a name for your note-gathering file.

Specifying your topic in this manner can save a great deal of "wheel-spinning" as you develop the presentation. It is imperative that you be able to clearly define what you will cover (and, by implication, what you won't) at this stage of your preparation.

Intent

Having specified your topic, you should ask yourself another vitally important question: "What can I reasonably expect to accomplish from this talk?" Put another way, "What, specifically, do I want from my listeners?" How will they respond?

Often your intent will be for the listener to *learn* or *do* something. Sometimes you may simply want to bring them up-to-date or even entertain them. The clearer your understanding of exactly what you are attempting, the greater your likelihood of success. In education, the modern approach is to set clearly measurable *learning objectives* (which I'll discuss in Chapter 12) so that teachers may recognize student achievements. The same might apply for most presentations in organizations. If a speaker's intent is unclear, unrealistic, or unproductive, that speaker is wasting the audience's time. Communicate for a specific desired response.

When specifying your intent, a note of caution may be called for. *Be realistic.* Even the most effective communicators do not always get all their listeners to respond as they would wish. Your listeners have minds of their own which sometimes resist what you are saying to them. They may view the topic in another light or simply won't agree with your proposal, no matter how clearly you express yourself. They may have varying degrees of susceptibility to your charms or your communication skills. And they may have values and attitudes which make it all but impossible to accept fully what you are advocating. This is especially true in persuasive situations.

As a general rule, it is easier to change a person's knowledge than it is to change his or her attitudes or behaviors. So, if your presentation is of a persuasive nature aimed at getting your listeners to *do* something they wouldn't normally do, your probability of total success is likely to be less than if your intent was simply to inform.

Examples of realistically stated intentions may be:

• I hope to get one sale for each 10 persons in the audience.

• I intend to get the boss to agree that we need a budget increase (even if she doesn't go for the full amount I have in mind.)

• I expect that the listeners will understand better how to interpret their monthly results printout accurately, thus reducing (but not eliminating) calls to the data processing supervisors.

Materials

Three categories of materials will affect your success: the physical environment, audio/visual support, and your notes and references. First, make the environment in which you are speaking conducive to your needs and to the needs of your listeners. Many physical elements can reinforce or detract from your presentation. If possible, check such things as the layout of the room, the furniture, the lighting, the temperature, the sound system, *before* you use the facility. If something isn't functioning properly or needs changing, you can correct it and avoid any last minute delays or surprises that can "rattle" your self-confidence.

Sometimes, of course, you have little control over the place where you'll give your pitch. If, for example, you are visiting someone else's office, it may be awkward to rearrange his furniture. But even here, there are some things you can do.

If you find yourself talking over a desk that seems like an imposing barrier, lure your listener around to your side with visual aids, a hands-on demonstration, or some other ploy. Or, ask if you could come around to his or her side so that you can show them important information. In a conference room or small group setting, get up and move around or even ask listeners to move their chairs around so they can better see your information which is important to them. Taking a few extra moments to set up a physical environment conducive to better communication is always worthwhile. Use of audio-visual devices often provides a good excuse for such rearrangement. This leads to the next category of materials, audio visual support.

Develop audio-visuals that amplify or reinforce the ideas presented orally. Charts, tables, graphs, handouts, sample equipment, films, slides, overhead transparencies, and the like should be gathered and used as appropriate. Whatever you decide to use, prepare it and practice with it in advance. We'll talk more about audio-visual support materials in Chapter 9. For now, let me simply make the point that we can do a great deal with effective audio-visual aids. Don't feel bound to the traditional flip chart, poster, or slide show. In your planning, think about the possible use of creative support materials for additional impact. Here is an example from a public relations presentation.

The speaker was faced with the prospect of explaining to his audience why the costs of drilling profitable oil wells was so high. He needed to get across the idea that computing the cost of profitable wells must be based on the cost of all the wells that are drilled in any one year rather than just the cost associated with those wells that were successful in producing oil. The problem was further complicated by the fact that different wells have different depletion rates and competition from other companies. His audience had little understanding of such concepts as "depletion" and "the high failure rate of finding productive oil wells." Part of the difficulty, of course, is that he was dealing with fairly abstract concepts. To bring his point home, he used a specially designed visual aid. ". . . the device is built on the punch board principle, with one hundred holes in a base board, over which hangs a metal plunger on a string." Listeners were invited to pick what they hope would not be a dry hole. (All except three holes are dry.) If they pick one of the three wells, a white light flashes on. If they hit one of the ninety-seven dry holes, a red light flashes on. The backboard of the display device bears basic information on the costs of drilling.[2]

This device allowed an opportunity for audience participation in the presentation. It also, of course, graphically illustrated the odds against hitting a productive oil well, the message the speaker was trying to get across.

A third class of materials is less tangible, but obviously very important: your information, notes and references. In every speaking situation, some research is needed. The quality of your ideas and information constitute the most important materials of all. Methods of gathering information, condensing, organizing it, and presenting it in such a way as to enhance credibility will be developed extensively later in this book. Good data do not speak for themselves; raw information must be organized into digestible and useful form. This leads us to the second M in TIMM'S CAT:

Message

This element refers to your plan of attack, the strategy for arranging the content of your message. Your message should be organized with a clear plan in mind. Assertions should be appropriately documented. The ideas presented should be directed toward your specific listeners—and the benefits to them should be clear.

The three essential parts to a well-planned talk are (1) an attention-gaining introduction, (2) a logically organized body of information, and (3) an action-oriented conclusion which seeks to have the listener try out or practice the intended behavior or way of thinking. I'll spend considerably more time on these items later in the book.

One very important point to keep in mind: In most briefing situations, the speaker need *not* be tied to an "I talk, you listen" format. Listener participation can be a key ingredient in getting your ideas across successfully. One common approach uses audience involvement following the body of your talk, keyed to getting the listeners to apply the ideas you've presented. Trainers and teachers frequently do this. Sometimes, however, it is useful to get your listeners involved earlier—perhaps by having them respond to some ideas before you present the main part of your message. This gets them thinking along appropriate lines. Everyone likes to participate, and the speaker who can get his or her listeners into the act is always that much more interesting to them.

Occasionally we are hesitant to use audience involvement in presentations. I can think of a personal example. While still fairly new at consulting, I was asked to do a training session for an organization of businessmen. I felt that I should *"teach,"* that is, *"tell"* them a lot of information. After all, I was being paid good money for teaching. Despite a carefully prepared module of instruction and the use of some of my best one-liners, the presentation seemed relatively unsuccessful. (My ego won't allow me to say it was a real flop.) Afterwards, a colleague who also worked with this group gave me some very good advice. He reminded me that my listeners were business people who are already very successful in their own fields. He went on to explain that they are often more interested in demonstrating their abilities to each other than in being taught in the traditional sense. The trainer, he advised, should *manage* the learning process, not force-feed information. I later revised the same program to include lots of listener interaction, cases and "experiential learning activities" (academic jargon for games) which allowed participants to "show off their stuff" while I more subtly interjected key learning objectives. The change in audience response was dramatic. The moral of the story: just because you're the "speaker" doesn't mean you should do all the talking.

One further thought on audience involvement is offered by Frederick C. Dyer. "When in doubt, schedule *twice* as much participation as seems adequate. Most speakers err on the side of too little participation rather than too much. The audiences love it; they enjoy it; they will never protest against too much talking or action on their part, but they will regret too little. One often sees speaker evaluation sheets with the comment, 'not enough group participation; too much monologue.' One never sees the comment, 'too much group participation.' "[3]

Summaries

Another key ingredient of the oral presentation is the use of summaries. Summaries tie together main points and help the listener organize and assimilate the ideas presented. Plan to use them liberally in your presentations. After making three or four main points, restate those points in a different way to keep them in the audience's mind. Few people can grasp and remember ideas the first time they're heard. We are by nature poor listeners. Some experts estimate the average person's listening effectiveness at about 25 percent. We *really listen* to only about a quarter of what we hear! To improve the probability your listeners will get your message, use internal summaries to tie together clusters of three or four points. Repetition is an extremely important learning device. Public speakers have long recognized the impact of the repeated idea.

Ralph Woods tells this story:

When a successful public speaker was asked the secret of his popularity, he said that it was really quite simple. "I tell them what I am going to tell them, then I tell them what I told them I was going to tell them, and then I tell them what I have told them."[4] Preview the message, present the message, and *summarize* the message.

Check-up

The check-up ingredient fulfills two purposes: (1) It helps you find out what the audience has learned, and (2) It provides valuable feedback about weaknesses in your presentation skills so that you can improve.

You might feel that testing for audience understanding is inappropriate or even impossible in a business presentation. After all, this isn't school where a teacher administers a pop quiz. Maybe not. But let's consider another view. If your topic is important enough to the organization and its members to present in the first place, it's certainly important enough to test for understanding.

Often, this testing phase requires creativity and perhaps a heightened sensitivity to your audience's responses. Here are a few techniques for checking-up that I've found useful.

1.   Ask questions and encourage feedback by responding positively to answers given, and relating the responses to the points you made in the presentation. Use questions which require thoughtful responses. The standard, "Are there any questions?" is not recommended simply because it often fails to generate meaningful comments. (You too often get a "no.") You might

instead ask, "How does your department handle . . . ?" or "In what ways could you best apply this information on the job?" *Be sure to respond to your audience's responses.* Comments like "I agree" or "good point" go a long way toward encouraging further responses. Even if the comment doesn't make much sense to you, at least thank the respondent for his thoughts. The worst thing we can do is let a person's comment just hang there in a silent vacuum. This will inevitably extinguish further interaction.

2.   Study the non-verbal responses of your listeners while you are talking. If you see uncertainty written on a face or if gestures or nods indicate agreement, use these signs as springboards for your questions. Be sure to do this in a nonthreatening manner and be sincere in your desire to have your listeners understand. In response to a nod of agreement you might say, "Tom, you look like you've had similar experiences. Would you like to share your thoughts with us?" If a listener appears to be confused, we might tactfully say, "Carol, I get the feeling I haven't explained this too well. How can I clear it up for you?"

3.   If the audience has been asked to learn the components that make up something, you can review their knowledge by holding up a chart and asking them to identify the components.

4.   Invite audience participation in reviewing what was learned by asking someone to demonstrate or summarize what you've presented.

Again, your only real limitation is your creativity. You owe it to your audience and yourself to determine what has been accomplished by your talk. What you learn from an effective check-up can be very useful in improving this presentation or future ones.

Assignment

Why not go a step beyond check-up and assign your listeners a little *homework?* It can easily be done, and most people won't even fight it. The effective assignment will give the audience something to remember about the presentation even after they have left the gathering. And that, of course, is the reason for its use. To be effective, appeal to their needs, interests, and desires. Show them how they can benefit from continued application of your ideas. Here are some assignments you might give an audience.

1.   Ask them to set up their own testing ground by trying out your ideas. Show an interest in hearing how their results turn out. Encourage them to tell you about their experiences.

2.   Ask them to look for situations each day at work which illustrate what you presented to them.

3. If your organizational position permits it, have the listeners report back to you about the implementation of your proposals.
4. Recommend other sources where they can learn more about the topic, such as through articles, books, or movies.
5. Suggest places where they can obtain further "teaching" on the subject, such as attending a workshop or joining a professional group.
6. Extend a challenge to try something new for a short period of time so that they can personally experience its benefits.

Take-Home

Now that you've assigned some "homework," you can further reinforce your presentation by giving the audience something *tangible* to take with them to remind them of your message.

The logic of providing some sort of handout to your audience is similar to that of the assignment step. Take-home items can keep on teaching after you're gone. These items can be of many forms, including samples, outlines, charts, letters, brochures, or badges. They may incorporate a mail-back card or sheet which further tests your listeners' grasp of the presentation. Take-home items serve as reminders and as sources of clarifying or amplifying information. These provide message reinforcement for those who use them and may be advertising for others who did not hear your talk. They also help overcome one of the disadvantages of oral presentations mentioned in Chapter 1: the lack of written information for further study.

Be sure take-home items are pertinent to your topic and intent. I've seen speakers pass out very attractive copies of case studies or articles which have little bearing on what was presented in their briefing. Also, be sure the quality of the handouts is appropriate in appearance and content. Take-home items should be selected very carefully for the particular audience. It may be useful to maintain a "family resemblance" in things you give out; a familiar logo or slogan may be repeated on each printed item to show that these go together and are not simply a hodge-podge of miscellaneous materials we had lying around.

Call attention to your take-home items during your presentation and explain them in terms of what good they'll be to your audience. Do *not,* however, pass out reading materials while you are speaking or you'll lose your audience. Often it may be appropriate to tie in the take-home with *check-up* and *assignment* phases of your presentation.

So, these are the planning elements of TIMM'S CAT. Hopefully, these will remind you that getting ideas across is seldom restricted in format like the formal public speech. You have a lot of room for creativity and listener involvement.

LISTENER INVOLVEMENT

At the risk of sounding like a broken record, let me reiterate one point. If there is any one ingredient that is crucial to effective presentations, it is *listener participation*. In some cases, this participation can be only a mental activity. But often—far more often than many speakers seem to realize—there are countless opportunities for audience involvement that slip by because of a traditional adherence to "I talk; you listen" format. But just don't take my word for it. From your own experiences, you undoubtedly have noticed that participatory communication experiences are far more rewarding and satisfying than those in which the audience is talked to. More learning takes place in a classroom where questions and discussion are encouraged than in one where only lectures are given. So, too, with getting your ideas across. Don't be afraid to involve your listeners!

Figure 2-1 is a conceptual planning checklist that will help you jot down some key thoughts. Use it to apply the material in this chapter. Another copy is found in the Appendix. You may want to make photocopies of it for future use.

CONCEPTUAL PLANNING:
THE BROAD STROKES

Chapter 2. A Summary of Key Ideas

1. Business presentations exist to answer questions and provide clarifying information.
2. Three classes of presentations are discussed. The *persuasive* presentation seeks conviction and action (mental or physical) from listeners. The *instructional* or *explanatory* talk provides the listener with information in a teaching context. *Progress reports* update listeners about developments relevant to a project or ongoing program they are already aware of.
3. The smaller the audience, the greater one's opportunities for tailoring remarks to specific listeners. Not all audience members may be equally important to the achievement of the goals of the talk.
4. TIMM'S CAT is an acronym to be used as a memory aid. It identifies the conceptual planning ingredients *T*opic, *I*ntent, *M*aterials, *M*essage, *S*ummaries, *C*heck-up, *A*ssignment, and *T*ake-home.
5. Listener participation is crucial to effective presentations.

FIGURE 2-1
Conceptual planning: applying "TIMM'S CAT" to your presentation

1. TOPIC: Give your talk a label or a working title to help identify the message. Be sure your title indicates the importance of the topic to your audience.

2. INTENT: Specifically, what do you want your audience to learn, think, do, or feel? What are your learning objectives? Be realistic but do state your goals in some measurable way if possible. Include secondary reasons for giving the talk (create favorable image, etc.)

3. MATERIALS: How will you attempt to arrange the physical environment? What audio-visual aids will you use? Will you use notes or a manuscript to help you remember key points? What might be some creative alternatives to what you've been doing in the past?

4. MESSAGE: How will you get your listener's attention? What appeals will you use? How will you build the need development stage of your talk? How will you arrange the key ideas of your talk? What kind of action step will you use? Sketch out a brief outline.

5. SUMMARY: How will you use summaries to help your listeners remember your key points? Can certain ideas be clustered together? Can you use some sort of memory aids to help retention? (TIMM'S CAT is a memory aid).

6. CHECK-UP: Name several ways you can check up on what the audience has learned. Be creative and specific.

7. ASSIGNMENT: What kinds of assignments might be effective for your presentation? How can you get the audience to keep on thinking about your talk? How can you get them to try new behaviors?

8. TAKE-HOME: What items can you give your listeners that will keep on teaching after you've gone? How can you make these useful? How can you create a "family resemblance" among these items?

9. WHAT CAN YOU DO TO INCREASE LISTENER INVOLVEMENT IN WHAT YOU ARE SAYING? Specifically, how will you strive for more participation?

NOTES

1. The acronym TIMM'S CAT has been previously published in Paul R. Timm, *Managerial Communication: A Finger on the Pulse* (Englewood Cliffs, NJ: Prentice-Hall, 1980), Chapter 7.

2. Edward J. Robinson. *Communication and Public Relations* (Columbus, Oh: Charles E. Merrill, 1966), p. 213.

3. Frederick C. Dyer. *Executive's Guide to Effective Speaking and Writing* (Englewood Cliffs, NJ: Prentice-Hall, 1962), p. 36.

4. Ralph L. Woods. *The Modern Handbook of Humor* (New York: McGraw-Hill, 1967), p. 460.

3

ANALYZING YOUR LISTENERS:

educated guesses

OBJECTIVES OF CHAPTER 3

After studying this chapter, the reader should be able to

1. Explain the importance of careful listener analysis to the effectiveness of a presentation.
2. Identify several approaches to listener analysis and some of the specific questions raised by each.
3. Explain why listener analysis is an ongoing process which starts with earliest planning, goes on through the delivery of the talk, and concludes only after post-presentation data is gathered.
4. Name five specific ways to gather listener analysis data.

William Penn said, "Better say nothing than not to the purpose. And to speak pertinently, consider both what is fit, and when it is fit to speak." But how do we determine "what is fit" so that we might speak "pertinently"? The answer to this lives within our listeners. The more skillful we become at determining what is pertinent to our listeners, the more effective we will be in communicating.

Listener analysis means making guesses based on as much information as we can reasonably gather.* From these guesses we can determine how best to formulate our message for maximum impact. The process is not mysterious; we all make guesses about others' behaviors every day. When we walk down a busy street we guess that others will go to one side of the sidewalk or the other. We anticipate the possibility that the person walking in front of us may suddenly stop to look in a shop window. More to the point, when we bring a message to someone, we picture mentally how that person is likely to react. When we inform our spouse that mother is coming to visit for a month or that the kitchen sink is clogged up again we can pretty well predict the kind of reaction we'll get. Professionally, we learn to predict responses. The orthodontist learns to anticipate the response to the announcement that Sandra needs braces. Sales representatives anticipate buyer objections ("It'll only get 16 miles to the gallon") and have carefully-prepared responses ("But with its larger gas tank, the Speedfire V-8 can go over 500 miles between fillups!").

---

*Although the more data available, the better our guesses are likely to be, there is a point at which any additional information would simply cost too much to get. For example, you could, theoretically, administer a battery of psychological tests to all the listeners before you talk to them. But this is seldom likely to be worth the costs in time and effort.

Listener analysis and the prediction of responses is a normal and natural activity for people in all walks of life.

But how do you learn to predict listener responses *accurately?* Usually through some combination of two elements: (1) your experiences with similar situations, and (2) your understanding of the actions, thoughts, values, and emotions of your listeners, or other people who are similar to your listeners. Of course, since each communication situation and each person is unique; we cannot predict with 100 percent accuracy. But we can profitably look for common characteristics likely to be found in most elements. Several approaches to audience analysis are suggested, a combination of which will generally yield the best results. Remember, audience analysis is a *questioning* process. The answers aren't always clear, yet the process is essential to effective communication.

MR. TWEEDY by Ned Riddle

"You're not still sore that we voted you 'Least Likely To Succeed' in Eastside High, are you, Ed?"

Listener analysis means making guesses about the predispositions of our audience based on all available information

Source: Copyright © 1979, Los Angeles Times Syndicate. Reprinted with permission.

THE "WHAT DO THEY NEED OR WANT TO KNOW?" APPROACH

You've been asked to give an oral briefing on a rather broad topic, say "technological developments in office equipment." Obviously you can't say everything there is to say about such a topic. So, you choose from the mass of available information some facts you think will be useful and interesting. Hopefully, you didn't select these solely on the basis of your interests; you attempted to anticipate your *listeners'* interests, too. This is a first step in this approach to audience analysis: making careful guesses about listener *interests* and *information needs.* These guesses are based on what you know about the listeners or others like them. For our example, say that in earlier presentations you've done, you perceived the strongest audience interest was in "power typing equipment." In your conversations with other managers in your organization they've expressed a need for facsimile transmission devices. You have recently attended an "office of the future" trade show where you saw equipment that could solve problems people in your organization have. Ideas of what material to cover can be distilled from these kinds of data.

Second, you need to have a good idea *how much they already know* about the subject you will talk about. You will lose your audience fast if you tell them what they already know; they'll feel you are insulting their intelligence. On the other hand, it is just as fatal to your presentation to talk about complex information to people who don't yet know the basics. Listeners who are, for example, totally unfamiliar with computer technology need to be brought up to date on exactly what small computing systems can do before they're likely to get very excited about purchasing one. This seems self-evident, yet I've seen several presentations by computer specialists who failed to answer the central question I had: "What exactly can I do with this?"

Third, you must find out *how much detail they want or need to know* about the topic. Giving detailed information to people who just want an overview of the material may annoy or bore them. Often, executives need abbreviated information or the picture painted with broad strokes. When a listener needs to know what time it is, don't tell him how to build a watch.

The organizational communicator has a distinct advantage over the public speaker in such audience analysis. To get clear answers to these questions, we can often simply go to the people we will be speaking to and ask them! We can also draw from our day-to-day interaction with them at work to get important clues about their predispositions, values, needs, and the like.

THE "WHAT DO THEY EXPECT?" APPROACH

Expectations have a way of being self-fulfilling. People hear what they expect to hear, even if they have to distort the speaker's real message to make it fit what they anticipated. Communication scholar Marshall McLuhan put it this way, ". . . There is a peculiar fact that whenever we encounter the unfamiliar we instantly translate it into the familiar and thereby never see the unfamiliar. People never see their environments. They never know them. They always know the preceding one. This stands out loud and clear."

When your message coincides with what the listener expected, your probability of communicating accurately is enhanced, unless your listener makes an "I've heard this all before" assumption. In such cases, details of your message may be lost since your listener feels he or she already knows what you are saying. If your message presents a point of view very different from what your audience expects from you, it pays to clarify early in the talk the fact that this may not be the message they anticipated.

How do these expectations arise? In businesses, one's organizational role provides clues as to the kinds of messages you are likely to produce. For example, a sales representative is probably going to try to sell you something while a labor leader will talk about employee needs that are not being met by management. Women executives may be expected to discuss problems unique to women workers while the guy from the computer center is expected to talk in technical and often hard to understand computer-speak. All these are, of course, stereotypes which may be false. The point is, a person's organizational role provides a preview of what we can expect them to talk to us about. When these expectations are not met—the hard-nosed assembly line foreman gives a humorous pitch about the company picnic or the union leader encourages sacrifices to improve productivity—the results can take us by surprise.

Personality characteristics, past behavior, personal appearance, age, sex, ethnic origin, race and countless other factors provide clues which we translate into expectations. The leader interested in getting across ideas that vary from these expectations may need to shock his audience into a recognition that the unexpected is being presented. The sales representative may open her pitch with the sincere statements: "I'm not here to sell you anything today. In fact, I won't even accept an order from you." This is likely to cause the purchasing agent to re-adjust his expectations and prepare for an unusual type of presentation. Similarly, the systems analyst who announces that he's "not here to talk about computers" may spark curiosity as well as adjust listener expectations.

It pays to ask yourself, "What does my audience expect from me?" If your topic is consistent with what they're likely to anticipate, use this to strengthen your message. If your topic is quite different, be sure to help them re-adjust their expectations lest they mentally distort your message and miss the point entirely.

THE "NATURE OF THE AUDIENCE" APPROACH

Although the term "audience" may conjure up an image of a public speaking situation, it need not be limited to that context. I've been using the word synonymously with listeners. When a group of listeners come together at a predetermined time and place for the purpose of information sharing, we have an audience. Certain roles generally emerge in such situations. Audience members normally accept the role of a listener; they are quiet and defer to the speaker. The speaker recognizes his or her role as the one making the utterances. In reality there is a lot more interaction—the two-way communication—going on than may meet the eye. The alert listener is carrying on a mental dialog with the speaker and with his or her own thoughts. The speaker is receiving nonverbal feedback from listeners in the form of facial expressions, body movement and laughs, grunts or yawns. And finally, there is interaction between the audience members. The listener who sees others dozing off, or becoming agitated, or enthusiastic may find her own reactions affected. Whispered remarks or snickers among audience members can quickly degrade the effectiveness of a serious presentation.

The type of audience we face affects these roles. William Brooks[1] identifies several different types of audiences. First among these is the casual audience which he also refers to as the *pedestrian* audience. An example of this may be shoppers who momentarily watch or listen to a demonstration of a particular product in a department store.

A second type of audience, and one the manager is more likely to deal with, is the *passive* or *partially oriented* audience. This type is often made up of captive listeners, people who have been invited and perhaps required to attend.

A third type of audience is the *selected* audience. This audience is composed of people who have gathered for some purpose which they clearly understand. Usually the audience here has been especially invited to the meeting because they have some sort of an interest in the proceedings or expertise.

A fourth audience is the *concerted* audience which has an active purpose. This audience has a clear understanding of why they've come together and is actively engaged in accomplishing some sort of clearly defined goals.

A fifth and final type of audience described in Brooks' text is the *organized* audience. This might be typified by an athletic team, a military unit, or a department within a business organization. Members of this type of audience are completely oriented toward the speaker. That is, the speaker enjoys considerable control over the audience in that they recognize him or her as the leader in this particular briefing.

Understanding what type of audience you will be dealing with can be useful in determining your primary emphasis. If you face a pedestrian audience, your first, and crucial task, is to gain your listeners' *attention*. Fail in this, and they'll simply leave! The passive audience is less likely to walk out on you, but you need to gain their *interest* in the topic very early or they'll mentally tune you out. For selected audiences there is generally some degree of interest already established. Here, you need to make a favorable impression and establish *credibility* early in the process. For the concerted or organized audience, your primary task is to elicit understanding, commitment, and specific *action*.

Although real audiences do not always fit so neatly into these categories (for example, two "selected" audiences could differ in many respects), the point of this thought-provoking approach is that as audiences become more or less polarized (in favor or against your position) the communicator's task is quite different. You can be more effective and efficient by getting to the pertinent point, so long as your analysis is accurate.

THE DEMOGRAPHIC APPROACH

The demographic approach to audience analysis gathers as much information as possible about certain key characteristics of the people you are speaking to. These characteristics may include such things as age, sex, socio-economic status, political philosophy, occupation, hobbies and activities, educational level and so forth. From these data, the speaker can draw certain inferences about the probable values and attitudes of his or her listeners. Let's consider several of these demographic characteristics.

1.   *Age.* A businessman presenting a briefing to a group of young employees should probably structure his message differently than to older employees. A number of studies have indicated that younger people tend to be more frequently idealistic, more impatient, and often more optimistic than older people. Older employees have a stronger tendency to think in terms of past experiences. They often consider new ideas in light of past failures and may prematurely write off a suggestion with, "We've tried that before, and it didn't work." Researchers conclude that, "As a general rule, it is suggested that a young audience will respond well to challenges and exciting new ideas while an older audience will respond more favorably to appeals to tradition and to moderate reforms with extensive practical justification."[2]

In addition to adjusting the content of your message in the light of your audiences' average age, the delivery might also be adjusted. In general, older people tend to prefer a slower, more deliberate style of speaking perhaps with more documentation and less emotionalism. The younger audience will tend to prefer a faster, more lively pace. In addition, younger employees tend to have higher dependence on visual information presentations. Having been raised in the television generation, they are used to seeing information as well as just hearing it. Audio-visual aids are often necessary to hold their attention.

2.   *Sex.* Many communication studies have determined that male listeners and female listeners respond differently to the same message. While rapidly

changing sex roles cast some doubt on the current validity of this research, past studies have indicated a general tendency for women to be more easily persuaded than men. Some evidence suggests that men tend to reason more objectively while women are more responsive to emotional appeals. Women have also been shown to retain more specific information about a particular message than do men.

3. *Socio-economic status.* A good communicator must consider the capability of an audience to understand his or her message. Individuals from lower socio-economic classes tend to have more difficulty in understanding complex information. Our capabilities for understanding are based on our experiences. An individual who was raised in a socially deprived situation has had considerably different experiences than the educated person from a more advantageous social background.

Clare W. Graves has developed a theory which suggests that people live at different "levels of existence." "At any given level, people exhibit behaviors and values characteristic of people at that level; a person who is centralized at a lower level cannot even understand people who are at a higher level."[3]

Put another way, most of us who are in leadership positions tend to view the world as a fairly pleasant place where we have opportunities for continued growth. Many workers, however, tend to view their lives from a less optimistic perspective. They see the future as an endless continuation of the humdrum present.

In communicating with such people, appeals to self-actualization or the gratifications of personal growth are likely to fall on deaf ears. They'll understand your words but will reject the notion that something positive could happen to them.

Such demographic characteristics as age, sex, socio-economic class, and so forth are not, of themselves, significant to the communicator. Their significance lies in the fact that *these things affect listener values and attitudes, which, in turn affect, in a very literal sense, the way they hear messages.* New incoming information is filtered through listener predispositions to determine if it makes sense. And if it is deemed sensible, is it pleasant, neutral or unpleasant to the audience. The result will be an audience that is either positive, neutral (disinterested), or negative towards the information you present.

When your audience is neutral or indifferent to what you have to say, your primary concern is to get them interested. Failing this, you run the risk that the audience will tune out as soon as they hear the topic. Indifferent listeners are likely to ask themselves, "What's in this for me?" or "Why do I need to know this information?" In such audience situations, the presenter takes on the role of an instructor; he or she must teach the audience how this information is of value to them.

When dealing with hostile listeners another problem arises. The speaker presenting information to such an audience should be aware that attitude change comes about rather slowly, and that the speaker should be realistic about the goals for a presentation. The more useful general technique in dealing with a potentially hostile audience is to establish some sort of common ground on which the audience and the speaker can agree at the value level. Fairly often you'll find that the speaker and audience do agree on the *ends* to be attained, but not on the *means*. Your audience is likely to have some expectations about how your message will come across. You need to be realistic in recognizing that to the hostile audience you will be viewed as one with low credibility. You have two strikes against you, but you're not out yet. If they expect your message to be bad—to communicate information they don't want to hear or they disagree with—you may be able to improve your situation if you are sensitive to this expectation.

Socialist Norman Thomas, who has faced many a hostile audience recommends ways of handling such situations:

"You don't insult your audience, but you may kid it; you don't patronize it or talk down to it; you don't apologize to it for your convictions; you don't whine about being "misunderstood"; you don't beg for favor. You assume and may occasionally appeal to an audience's spirit of fair play, its sporting instinct, its desire to know what you think. You seek a point of contact— sometimes by sharp challenge to arouse attention, sometimes by beginning with partial agreement with what you assume is majority sentiment and then on that basis developing your divergence in thinking. You try—but not too often or too hard—to appeal to your audience's sense of humor even in divergence of opinion. If the facts warrant it, and you have led up to it, you may denounce specifically and vigorously ideas and actions with which large sections of your audience have been in accord. But be sure of your facts and be very sparing in imputing to your opponents base motives. In the minds of some men, honest, well supported denunciation may stick and bring forth later fruit."[4]

The potentially hostile audience calls for special sensitivity—and courage. Some research has shown that if the communication is only slightly better than expected by the audience, hope may dominate and the message may be distorted in the listener's mind in an overly favorable way.

In other words, if you go into the hostile or unpleasant communication situation and you can provide the audience with a message less negative than it expects, you may come out with a favorable audience response.

In dealing with an audience that is already favorable toward you, the main goal of the speaker will be to reinforce and intensify the positive attitudes they now hold. Often this group will be motivated by relatively emotional appeals. The listeners will be far more tolerant of imperfections in your presentation. Emotional appeals work better here than they would among hostile or neutral groups.

Demographic characteristics of your audience provide clues about their attitudes, values, abilities and interest; their view of the world. As you become sensitive to this view, you can adapt your message to it and greatly improve the probability of successful communication.

LISTENER ANALYSIS DURING THE PRESENTATION

We've focused thus far on educated guesses we can make about how our listeners will respond. The effective communicator makes audience analysis an *ongoing process,* before, during and after the presentation. The sensitive speaker will get a great deal of information from his or her listeners as the presentation is given.

Often this information is nonverbal in nature, such things as apparent attentiveness, facial expressions, a general sense of restlessness, excitement, passiveness, or apathy. All of these kinds of things convey to the speaker whether or not he or she is coming across effectively. The trick, of course, is to adapt and adjust to this feedback so that you hold your audience's interest. As we will discuss later in the book, such things as physical movement, gestures, and voice changes can do a great deal to animate and make your presentation more lively. In addition, and more importantly, gaining audience involvement through mental or physical participation is crucial to communication success.

Build flexibility into any presentation. We can never predict exactly the reactions of our listeners, so be prepared to take a different tack if the feedback you get from your ongoing analysis tells you the audience needs a change.

POST-PRESENTATION LISTENER ANALYSIS

Immediately upon completion of your presentation you are likely to get some very valuable feedback. The most common type of post-presentation analysis is the immediate, overt audience response. Such things as applause, questions, compliments and criticisms from audience members will help the speaker gauge his or her effectiveness. In addition to this, many speakers find it useful to get more structured feedback in the form of questionnaires, written comments or specific speaker critiques from trusted associates. These can be very helpful.

Although it is too late to change the presentation you've just given, these kinds of information can be beneficial in determining how to prepare your next presentation. Every speech experience, if evaluated constructively, can add to the speaker's repertoire of skills and understanding of audiences and form a basis for more sophisticated, sensitive audience analysis in the future.[5]

Ask for feedback from others whose judgment you trust. But be ca. *how* you ask. Don't just fish for compliments; seek constructive criticism too.

"Know thy audience" should be the motto of anyone sincerely interested in being a better communicator. Effort expended in a careful, probing analysis of your listeners will pay handsome dividends in helping you speak pertinently and to the purpose. To help structure your questioning approach, Figure 3-1, a listener analysis checklist, is provided below.

FIGURE 3-1
Listener analysis checklist

1. State your major purpose. What, precisely, do you want to happen in *this* audience as a result of your talk?

2. What specific advantages can you offer to this audience if they listen to you?

3. How much do they already know about your topic?

4. How resistant are they likely to be to your ideas? Why?

5. What kinds of evidence or information will likely be well received?

6. How can you find out more useful audience analysis information?

ANALYZING YOUR LISTENERS

Chapter 3. A summary of key ideas

1. Listener analysis is a questioning process which seeks to predict audience reponses to our message.
2. One approach asks questions about listener interest and information needs in regard to the proposed message. It seeks to find out what

information is needed, how much is already known, and how much detail is required.

3. Another approach focuses on expectations of listeners. It asks, "What do they expect from my presentation?" Anticipating and building upon listener expectations can improve the probability of successful communication. Misjudging expectations can result in listeners being turned off to your message.

4. Another listener analysis approach studies the nature of the audience. Audiences may be categorized as pedestrian, passive or partially oriented, selected, concerted, or organized. Each type calls for a slightly different emphasis, especially in the opening moments of a presentation.

5. A final approach looks at demographic characteristics of listeners. From such characteristics as age, sex, socio-economic status, speakers can draw inferences about responses to their message. The significance of demographic differences among people lies in their effect on listener values and attitudes, which, in turn, affect the way they hear messages.

6. Attitudes and values change very slowly. The credibility of a speaker can be crucial in bring about such changes even among hostile audiences if the message is viewed less negatively than anticipated.

7. Listener analysis should continue during and after the presentation. The effective communicator will be sensitive and responsive to audience feedback. Getting critiques from trusted associates after the talk can help improve future efforts.

NOTES

1. William D. Brooks, *Speech Communication,* 2nd ed. (Dubuque, Iowa: Wm. C. Brown, 1974), p. 259. Brooks' discussion is based on a system of audience analysis originally explained by H.L. Hollingsworth in *The Psychology of the Audience* (New York: American Book, 1935), p. 25.

2. Ibid., p. 265.

3. Clare W. Graves. "Human Nature Prepares for a Momentous Leap," *The Futurist,* April 1974, p. 72.

4. Norman Thomas. *Mr. Chairman, Ladies and Gentleman . . .* (New York: Heritage House, 1955), p. 116.

5. Brooks, op. cit., p. 284.

4

PREPARING YOUR MIND

OBJECTIVES OF CHAPTER 4

After studying this chapter, the reader should be able to:

1. Explain the concept of our "coping quotient" as it relates to speaker anxiety.
2. State three ways we can reduce the number of specific things competing for our attention in order to bring the communication situation comfortably within our coping quotient.
3. Explain five common pitfalls in language use which lead to faulty thinking and communicating.
4. Explain three approaches to reasoning and give examples of when each can be most profitably used.
5. Name the major pitfalls in inductive and deductive reasoning.
6. Explain how the Rogerian approach to reasoning can be applied by communicators.

The skillful communicator puts mind before matter. A great deal of mental spade work precedes an effective presentation. The previous two chapters have attempted to guide you through conceptual planning and contemplation of your audience. In this chapter we'll look further at mental activities underlying the preparation and presentation of a briefing, oral report, or persuasive talk. Three areas will be covered: (1) developing proper mental attitude, (2) being aware of pitfalls in language use, and (3) applying sound reasoning: the fine art of thinking it through.

DEVELOPING PROPER MENTAL ATTITUDE

Okay, it's probably been on your mind, so let's talk about it right now: speaker anxiety, also known as "stage fright."

The thought of giving a talk in front of others has a way of unraveling even self-confident individuals. Surveys have indicated that of all things people fear, giving a public speech tops the list. Comedian George Jessel once said, "The human brain is a wonderful organ. It starts to work as soon as you are born and doesn't stop until you get up to deliver a speech." President Jimmy Carter's wife Rosalyn once confided that she used to vomit before delivering each speech early in her husband's campaign.

The story is told of Edward Rickenbacker, the World War I hero recognized as the "Ace of Aces."

An important banquet was given in his honor. He stood up to a great ovation, opened his mouth to speak, and was terrified.

"He mumbled a few phrases in poor grammar and sat down. He decided right there and then that this would never happen to him again. The next day he hired a coach to teach him how to speak; he asked Damon Runyon to write him a speech; he studied grammar and arranged for a long lecture tour (at $1,000 a night) and thereby conquered his fear of speaking in public.

Mr. Rickenbacker learned that each specialty requires its own preparation. A hero in battle can be a coward at the banquet when he rises to speak, unless he is prepared.[1]"

Only a drunk or a fool is likely to be completely comfortable speaking before an audience. But the cure for anxiety is not to be found in a bottle. There are better ways to reduce such discomfort, but don't expect it to go away totally. That really isn't even desirable. Anxiety plays an important role in keeping us mentally alert.

YOUR COPING QUOTIENT

Communication professors Harold Zelko and Frank Dance suggest that, while recognizing the total absence of anxiety as both unrealistic and undesirable, we

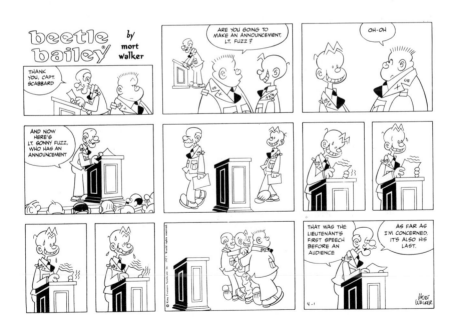

Source: Reprinted by permission of King Features Syndicate, Inc.

can develop our own "coping quotient" by reducing the number of things we must give conscious attention to. In other words, as aspects of presentational speaking become natural and spontaneous—almost unconscious—we can concentrate on the overall purpose of our briefing. It's like typing or playing a musical instrument. So long as we must consciously think about how each finger should be positioned to print a letter or produce a note, we will never be effective in putting together the entire composition.

There are several ways to reduce the number of specific things competing for your attention in order to bring the presentation comfortably within your coping quotient.[2]

1. *Prepare!* There is absolutely no substitute for adequate preparation. If you are well prepared, your capacity to cope with problems rises significantly. Nothing reduces anxiety like being well prepared to the point of being overprepared—totally confident of your grasp of the subject matter. Preparation should go beyond the content and delivery of the presentation to include practice in handling anticipated questions that may arise. Some suggest this rule of thumb: You should spend one hour of preparation for each minute of speaking. This includes research, conceptual planning, message development and practice.

2. *Be Idea-Conscious, Not Self-Conscious.* Having your specific purpose in mind helps reduce overconcern for irrelevant details. The principles of the "unconscious success mechanism" enters here. We are most effective when we don't think of each step or each procedure needed to complete a task but instead focus on the desired result and let our subconscious mind help us get there. The baseball outfielder going after a high fly ball doesn't consciously think, "I'll take six steps to my left, two steps forward, raise my glove with my left hand and shield my eyes from the sun with my right hand . . ." Instead he fixes his eyes on the ball and visualizes the desired result of catching it. His unconscious success mechanisms go through the process of bringing that to pass and free him from concerns about tripping over his shoelace, taking the wrong size steps or raising his glove too late.

The same principle applies in presentational speaking. Overconcern with mechanics once you've reached the point of doing the talk can only be distracting and anxiety-producing. Zelko and Dance give this example:

> Self-consciousness tends to be self-destructive. If you are overly worried about the way you look, you often overcompensate and this draws to yourself attention which would not ordinarily be centered on you. It's when you are trying to walk nonchalantly that you walk stiffly or affectedly. It is when you are trying to smile naturally (Say 'cheese') that your smile tends to look artificial. If you are caught up in a conversation or in telling a story and the conversation or the story causes you to smile, you are usually unaware of the smile itself, and it is at that point that the smile is, and appears, most natural. Similarly with speaking in

public. When you are caught up in the message of your speech, when you are interested in communicating the ideas of the speech to the listeners, you are not usually uncomfortable or noticeably concerned with how you look or how you sound—it's the idea that is at center stage, not the self. Simple remedies: Be audience-centered; be message-centered; not self-centered.[3]

3. *Relax.* If you are well prepared and idea-conscious, not self-conscious, you are raising your coping quotient to a level where anxiety should not be a problem. If you still feel that flush of nervousness just as you are being introduced, don't worry about it. It's perfectly natural and it is seldom visible to your audience. When you get up to speak, take a moment to arrange your notes, look at your audience and smile, and take a few slow, deep breaths.

Once you've had speaking experiences, your coping quotient quickly increases and you get to the point where you welcome the opportunity to stand up before a group with your well-prepared talk.

YOUR LISTENERS WANT YOU TO SUCCEED

I can think of very few circumstances in which your audience hopes your presentation will flop. When people have taken the time to assemble for the purpose of hearing what you have to say, they don't want to feel the time has been wasted. Even the hostile listener wants you to explain yourself clearly if for no other reason than that he can then attempt to shoot down your ideas.

Let's face it, a poor presentation can be just as embarrassing and uncomfortable for the audience as it is for the speaker. Sometimes even more so. The naive speaker may be unaware of a low quality talk, while his listeners may be embarrassed for him or her.

No one is out to get you. As Elmer Davis described it, "The first and great commandment is, 'Don't let them scare you.' " Your audience wants you to succeed.

HAVE SOMETHING WORTH SAYING

If you've applied principles of conceptual planning and listener analysis as suggested in this book, you'll clearly distinguish the topic worth speaking about. As a manager, you face frequent needs to communicate with others. Often the question isn't whether or not to communicate, but by what *medium* should you communicate. We've already discussed some of the decision criteria in Chapter One. A carefully prepared presentation costs money. So be sure you're not using a $100 medium to convey a 25¢ idea.

Occasionally we find that a person gets to where he or she enjoys speaking before groups—yes there are such people—so much that they'll take the opportunity even when they have little or nothing worth saying. James Russell Lowell said, "Blessed are they who have nothing to say and who cannot be persuaded to say it." If your purpose can be achieved in two or three minutes, don't feel obligated to use a half-hour. One anonymous wag criticized a speaker who "had a two-second idea, a two-minute vocabulary, and a two-hour speech." Abraham Lincoln said it best: "I believe I shall never be old enough to speak without embarrassment when I have nothing to talk about."

PITFALLS IN LANGUAGE USE

Let's assume you do have something to talk about and you've decided that an oral presentation is the appropriate medium. Even before you begin to gather notes or rough out an outline, another form of mental preparation is useful. We need to give some thought to the ways we use language. We use words for more than just giving voice to our messages; we also reason with words. Words are what we process as we think. And it is very helpful to recognize limitations of language and "the way we word."[4]

George deMare suggests that such careful pre-thought points out one way we can distinguish the amateur from the professional person: "The amateur always rushes out the work while it is still hot and the creative flush is upon him, only to be humiliated a week or so later to read in the cold light of day what he had sent forth into the world."[5]

Let's take a few minutes to look before we leap. A clearer understanding of how language works can be an effective vaccine against the dreaded communicator's disease: foot in the mouth.

LANGUAGE: A MAJOR SOURCE OF MISCOMMUNICATION

It may seem ironic that language—the very basis of what many view as real communication—poses one of the most pervasive sources of misunderstanding in our communicative processes. But it does.

I've made the point earlier that we all develop our own unique ways of using words and symbols in thinking and describing to others what we think. How we process and arrange words is our personal language *structure*. Our sensory experience—that is, our perceptions of the physical world to which we attach words and symbols—can be likened to data cards for a computer. And in these terms, our language structure is analogous to a system program, which tells the computer what to do with new data.

Language-caused miscommunications arise from both significant differences in the meanings people attach to experiences—we read the data cards differently—and from differences in ways we process the words—through our reasoning systems. There are two ways to improve language communication skills. We can either increase a person's vocabulary so that more precise "data cards" can be produced, or we can improve the match between language structures—the ways we reason with words—and objective reality. Increasing someone's vocabulary will usually be a far less fruitful approach than working on language reasoning unless there is a seriously inadequate vocabulary, such as when one is learning a new language or a lexicon of technical terms. A far more valuable approach to get at frequent communication breakdowns is to examine our logic and show discrepancies between the way we "process" words and the way the real world behaves.

Let's look at several assumptions about word use that cause some of the more common problems.

Confusing facts with assumptions. Many problems or miscommunication arise when the way we structure our language does not distinguish adequately between fact and assumption. And to presume that people in general, including ourselves, know an absolute fact when they see one is a dangerous presumption.

In truth, the vast majority of information we receive is inference or opinion, not fact. Something we personally observe or experience can be regarded as fact, at least for us. But just about anything else should be considered inference or opinion. *We run into misunderstanding and disagreement with others when we state assumptions as though they were facts.* The problem is that the language we normally use does not *automatically* make the distinction clear. So we must make an extra effort to do so.

For example, under normal circumstances, we can state direct observations—"I saw Tom leave the plant at five o'clock"—as facts. But if we take the fact about Tom leaving the plant and try to elaborate on it, what we say becomes an inference. For example, when we say, "I saw Tom leaving the plant *to go home,*" we are now adding a new dimension to the message that may or may not be true, in fact. That Tom left the plant can be verified by observation, but that he went home is merely inferential on our part, unless, of course, Tom's home is in view and we see him walk there.

An inference is a conclusion based upon incomplete information, and much of what we talk about is based on inference. By necessity, we communicate inferences all the time. But problems arise when our listeners are unclear as to whether we are inferring or speaking of fact. Our language tends to muddy this distinction, so inferences have a way of coming out sounding awfully factual.

Again, let me restate: There is nothing inherently wrong with drawing inferences. Inferences are necessary for people to make day-to-day sense of the world. We seldom have the luxury of having *all* available data at our disposal before we draw conclusions. The important thing is that we recognize inferences as such and that we word them in ways that will help us and our listeners avoid confusing them with facts. Failure to do so can often lead to confusion and argument.

There are ways to clarify an assumption and thus make it a factual statement. Adding a "to me" phrase will do this. Instead of saying "that new policy is foolish" we might say, "To me," or "I think the new policy is foolish." There's a big difference between the two forms of that statement. The first is an assumption, or in this case, an opinion, stated like a fact. The second is clearly identified as fact. The speaker is using a "to me" clarifier. It's a *fact* that *I think* the policy is foolish.

Think of how you'd respond to the above statements if you disagreed, if you felt the policy was not foolish. In the first form, the policy *is* foolish, you'd be likely to argue the point since you see it otherwise; in the second form, you'd perhaps disagree, but you'd recognize that as just one person's impression of the policy. Often, of course, an evaluative statement like the first one above is simply an expression of a personal preference and not a condemnation of the thing discussed. Nobody can argue with what you "like." If you say, "I don't like that decision," that's your right and other people will respect it. But if you say, "That was a rotten decision," then others may be put on the defensive if they liked the decision.

When an opinion is not identified as such, the receiver of the message has to make a decision on how to respond—whether to be "nice" and agree with you or to be true to his or her feelings and say that it was *not* a rotten decision. If contrary opinions are offered, the risk of starting an argument is increased and the probability of mutual understanding drops sharply. *Anything I say is a statement about me.* Whenever we make a statement we reveal something about ourselves. Friedrich Nietzsche said, "Every word is a preconceived judgment." We choose what we will say, as well as how we'll say it, on the basis of a personal system of values and attitudes. Here is an example.

If I state the opinion that "Vernon is stupid," it may appear on the surface that stupidity is an inherent characteristic of Vernon. But what, in fact, I am saying is that

- My personal experience has supplied me with a meaning for the word "stupid."
- I have perceived Vernon's behavior as fitting my view of the concept of "stupidity."
- Therefore, I have concluded that Vernon is stupid.

Notice that the words "I" and "me" enter into this analysis throughout.

When I conclude that Vernon is stupid, I am really talking about my own opinion. I've related these two things, Vernon and stupidity. *I* have related them within my world of words. Whether or not they are really related remains unclear.

So, in essence, every opinion we offer is a statement about ourselves. This is so because

> We can never say all there is we have to say about any topic, since this would take too long. Therefore . . .
>
> Those things we do choose to talk about and those that we choose to ignore involve a selection process on our part, based on our past experiences. Thus whereas . . .
>
> Each of us has had totally unique experiences—no two people have experienced the same things, and since . . .
>
> We have each created our own unique way of attaching words or labels to our world or experiences—therefore . . .
>
> When we combine several of these labels into a message, we are saying very little about what is "real" and instead are describing something that is of great importance to us personally.

Thus to conclude that, "Vernon is stupid," is to report on some word associations I have made. This statement doesn't really say much about Vernon, but it does say some interesting things about me.

Again, clarification of our point of view via some form of a "to me" qualifier adds accuracy to our statement. Failure to so clarify what our message is can lead to considerable embarrassment, incorrect conclusions, and serious harm to our credibility. I suspect this potential breakdown was in S.I. Hayakawa's mind when he said that general semantics—that is, the study of language and its behavioral effects—could more accurately be described as the study of "how not to be a damn fool."

Oversimplified categories. Another common problem in the way we structure language is the tendency to oversimplify the categories into which we mentally sort things. We deal with our life experiences like eggs in a carton, neatly fitting each experience into one of several compartments.

Many people rely too heavily on polar terms, words that force us to choose between extremes—like good or bad, weak or strong, big or little—and which tend to oversimplify and confuse. In reality, most things we encounter in life are more accurately described in terms of probabilities or fine variations among events or experiences than by an either-or category. In other words, our experiences represent some shade of gray, rather than black-or-

white differentiations. To illustrate, simply ask yourself—and others—
questions such as these:

1. Are you a good manager or a bad manager?
2. Are you big or little?
3. Are you liberal or conservative?
4. Are you handsome (pretty) or ugly?
5. Are you a success or a failure?

People often ask questions just as absurd as these. The appropriate
response, of course, would be compared to what (or whom)?

Don't let yourself get painted into a box with someone else's oversimplified questions. And if you're really interested in establishing
understanding—in really communicating—avoid these simplistic polar
terms. I recently saw a nationally prominent governor interviewed on television. The interviewer repeatedly asked a variation of the same question, "Did
you go to Washington, to dramatize a problem and serve the people of your
state, *or* to advance your own presidential ambitions?" The politician's answers
proved frustrating to the newsman and perhaps seemed to be evasive but the
question could not accurately be answered when cast in an either-or form.
Finally, the politician simply stated that he did not look at the world in such
simplistic black-white terms, and that there were many reasons behind his
actions. Probably the best answer in this case was, "both," although the
politician who had not yet announced his candidacy for president did avoid
that one.

For managers, the either-or reasoning pitfall can have serious effects.
One particular problem is the tendency to classify workers as industrious or
lazy or as productive or unproductive. In one company I've heard of, a sales
manager actually had a big chart on his office wall with the names of his
salesmen boldly displayed under the headings "Heros" and "Bums."

When our language and thinking utilize such either-or logic, other
possibilities are overlooked. If we only classify a manager as a good leader or
bad leader, we leave out a lot of other possibilities. Maybe he or she is effective
in some dimension of the job while ineffective in others.

Sales representatives and other persuaders often manipulate this either-
or orientation to their advantage. "Would you like to take delivery immediately or next week?" attempts to preclude the option of not taking
delivery at all. It's the old story of the ice cream shoppe owner who asked each
customer whether they wanted one egg or two in their milkshakes. Few people
said neither, and he charged extra for each egg, of course.

Our credibility can be seriously damaged when listeners recognize this
kind of oversimplified reasoning. While there are legitimately dichotomous
categories—such as present or absent—most things don't fit so neatly into

either-or slots. Or sometimes the categories themselves become so broad as to be meaningless. Whenever we hear ourselves or others sending either-or messages, it might be wise for us to consider.

- Are all the options covered?
- As compared to what (or whom)?

Self-fulfilling expectations. If we come to see our subordinates as either heroes or bums we are likely to have those perceptions verified. They will, in fact, become (or continue to be) heroes or bums. But this doesn't really make sense. We all know that people change. Today's hero may have been yesterday's bum—if we, as managers, have been able to avoid the related problem of self-fulfilling expectations. Because we usually choose what perceptions we will pay attention to and then mesh these things into our views of reality, there is a strong tendency to only look for the pieces that fit. We reject the possibility that the hero has done something seriously wrong or that the bum actually did a great job.

Similarly, there are interactive effects between our perceptions and the ways we talk. What we see directly affects what we say. And what we say in turn affects what we see. The filters of our mind develop over time as we label our world of experiences, and these filters then determine what we select to perceive. When we can make no sense of some thing or event—that is, if it doesn't fit our world view—we tend to reject it.

It can be quite disconcerting, for example, to find the worker we've labeled "rebellious" suddenly vigorously defending the status quo. It's also unsettling to find the "nice, pleasant" receptionist suddenly shouting angrily at a visitor. We'd prefer to reject or explain away such discrepancies because they just don't jive with "the way things are" in our mental worlds. The way we label things leads to expectations of how things will be in the future.

The supervisor who labels a subordinate lazy will undoubtedly find more and more evidence to support the judgment. And in all likelihood, this supervisor's attitude will then be perceived by the worker, thus leading to suspicion and distrust. The overall result is a strong potential for miscommunication. *So let's keep our labels, if we must use them, somewhat loose.* Let's build into them some flexibility so that unanticipated changes in things, events, and people can be plugged into our mental worlds without throwing us off balance.

The world is dynamic; language more static. Modern self-help techniques all begin with an important premise: *Each individual is unique and capable of change.* But problems of communication arise because although the world of experiences is dynamic and everchanging, the world of words is much less flexible. Language tends to change very slowly, leaving us with the problem of trying to describe fluctuating processes with words that stress consistencies.

People are also constantly in a process of change. As George Bernard Shaw once said, "The only man who behaves sensibly is my tailor; he takes my measurements anew each time he sees me, whilst all the rest go on with their old measurements and expect them to fit me." Failure to accept change leads to many communication difficulties. Psychologist Carl Rogers has suggested that, "If I accept the other person as something fixed, already diagnosed and classified, already shaped by his or her past, then I am doing my part to confirm this limited hypothesis. If I accept him or her as a process of becoming, then I am doing what I can to confirm or make real his or her potentialities." In other words, if I believe that the word labels I've attached to a person are not changeable, I cannot then cope with changes in that person.

Need for clear language use. To be credible as a message source, a person must be constantly aware of limitations posed by language. We need to remind ourselves frequently that words do not have inherent meanings. They are simply labels that we attach in unique and individual ways to our world of experiences. And since labels trigger meanings in others, the degree to which we achieve true communication is determined in part by how accurate we are in relating these labels to reality. If we are inaccurate, we described a world that is not there. Carried to the extreme, inappropriate language uses can affect our mental health. Our psychological and sociological well-being can depend upon our being aware of the important ways in which language reflects and influences the way we think and communicate.

Many communication problems arise from a lack of awareness about "the way we word." In fact, when the many pitfalls of language processing are pointed out, it seems amazing that people can communicate at all.

THE FINE ART OF THINKING IT THROUGH

T. DeVere White once described the ill-prepared communicator: "He discloses the workings of a mind to which incoherence lends an illusion of profundity." Perhaps we can, on occasion, get away with an "illusion of profundity"—but not for long. The business communicator has an obligation to be coherent and clear. The old adage, "when in doubt, mumble" won't work in an oral presentation.

Without getting too deeply into philosophy, there are some principles of logic and reasoning which can be reviewed profitably. Let's look at three important approaches to reasoning: inductive logic, deductive logic and the Rogerian approach. Applying these adds power to what you say.

INDUCTIVE REASONING

When using inductive reasoning, a person moves from observations or other evidence about *specific cases to a generalization about all such cases.* We use this kind of reasoning constantly. The question is, how effectively do we use it? When used responsibly, it is a powerful logical form. Some people, however, use it carelessly and thus brand themselves as sloppy thinkers. The most frequent pitfalls are generalizing (1) from too little evidence, (2) from poor quality or biased evidence, or (3) from irrelevant evidence. I am here using the term evidence synonymously with "data," "support," or "observations."

Suppose, for example, a manager drops into a small production shop unannounced at 10 a.m. and observes the following:

- one employee is drinking a cup of coffee in the rest area; he appears very sleepy
- one employee (who has a reputation for being a "goof-off") is repairing a child's bicycle
- two members of the work crew are absent, and
- the supervisor is talking on the phone to his wife
- no one appears to be doing any company work.

Many a manager would make a sweeping conclusion—the shop is not running right—which could lead to a serious, and perhaps unfounded, chewing out for the supervisor or employees. Such a manager may be guilty of faulty induction.

Although the above evidence may point to an obvious conclusion that something is wrong in the shop, there may be other, perfectly valid explanations. Using only these five observations to draw a conclusion is too little evidence. The worker repairing the bike already is a known goof-off (biased evidence) and the absentees and supervisor-on-the-phone data may be completely irrelevant. Several other facts could explain the observations and point to a totally different conclusion.

- This crew had worked all through the previous night to complete a rush project.
- The shop was participating in a "toys for kids" Christmas program by repairing donated items to distribute to needy children. Several workers have donated their own time and talents to this work using company facilities.
- Despite the excessive overtime just completed, two of the crew mem-

bers volunteered to help out in another department while their own workload was slack.

• The supervisor had not been home in two days and his wife has been nursing a sick child.

• The shop's normal work was stopped awaiting retooling.

Kind of changes the conclusion, doesn't it? The point, of course, is that obvious evidence does not always provide what we need for accurate inductive reasoning. Rhetorician Maxine Hairston suggests the following as minimum criteria for supporting data from which we inductively arrive at a conclusion.

1.   The evidence should be of sufficient *quantity*.
2.   The evidence should be *randomly selected*.
3.   The evidence should be *accurate* and should be *objective*.
4.   The evidence should be *relevant* to the conclusion drawn.[6]

In our example above, the manager's original conclusion was based on evidence that did not meet these criteria. Five observations, all gathered at one point in time, at least one of which was tainted by a preconceived low opinion of the person observed, led to an inaccurate conclusion.

One other major pitfall of inductive reasoning is the tendency to select and interpret evidence in such a way that it confirms a bias we already have. We've already discussed the concept of self-fulfilling expectations which can distort our reasoning. When using inductive reasoning, a common error is to hold *a priori* assumptions—premises formed before the evidence is examined. These presumptions cause us to select evidence that reinforces what we already think, and to ignore that which doesn't fit. This process cannot be called valid induction.

While it is unlikely that we could totally overcome these preconceived biases, raising them to the conscious mind and attempting to compensate for them in our data gathering will lead to more accurate, logical reasoning. The careful thinker seeks information which may go against the grain of her or his normal thought patterns.

As we reason from examples to a generalization we make an "inductive leap." Hairston concludes her discussion of induction by saying:

"Moving from an examination of some of the available evidence to a generalization about the whole population from which that evidence is drawn is known as the 'inductive leap.' If our sample is sufficient, random, accurate, and relevant, we can be confident that the leap is warranted. *If the sample does not meet these criteria, we are not reasoning, but jumping to conclusions.*"[7] (italics added)

DEDUCTIVE REASONING

While inductive reasoning arrives at a general conclusion based on specific evidence, *deductive* reasoning *takes generalizations and applies them to new cases.* For example, much research has led to the conclusion that computers save time. Deductive reasoning would start from that generalization and reach a new conclusion applicable to a specific instance—a computer will save time *in our business.* In many cases, no support is expressed for the initial assumption (computers save time) because that conclusion (which was originally arrived at by inductive logic) is taken for granted. That statement becomes a "given." Deduction now builds upon that by looking to a specific case. The question is, "Does the general conclusion apply in our specific and, perhaps unique, situation?"

Deductive reasoning is based in a logical form of argument called a *syllogism.* Most of us are familiar with the classical expression of syllogisms where both premises and the conclusion are clearly stated. You may recall from philosophy classes

Major premise: All men are mortal.

Minor premise: Socrates is a man.

Conclusion: Socrates is mortal.

In day to day use, our syllogisms are usually abbreviated with one or more of the premises or the conclusion left unspoken. Harold Janis shows how the form changes in normal conversation. In formal logic, the syllogism would be:

Major premise: All our employees are covered by group insurance.

Minor premise: Joe Ford is an employee.

Conclusion: Joe Ford is covered by group insurance.

In conversational reasoning, we'd be more likely to say, "Joe Ford must be covered by group insurance because he's an employee" (major premise omitted); or "Joe Ford is covered by group insurance" (major premise and minor premise omitted).[8] Although we seldom use formally expressed syllogisms in business presentations, we can and should use them to test the validity of our deductive arguments. The validity depends on the syllogism's ability to meet three criteria:

1. The premises must be true.
2. The major premise must include all cases.

3. The premises must be so related that they lead invariably to the conclusion.[9]

Here is an example of a syllogism that does *not* meet these criteria.

Major premise: Oil company executives are greedy.
Minor premise: Mr. Roscow is greedy.
Conclusion: Mr. Roscow is an oil company executive.

This, of course, is absurd since the major premise is not always true, the minor premise is subject to argument and the conclusion does not follow from the premises. The above example is called *categorical syllogism* because the major premise makes an unqualified assertion about all members of a class. Other forms of syllogism are often more subtle and a bit tougher to check for validity.

The *disjunctive syllogism* states alternative possibilities in the major premise and then separates a specific case into one of the alternatives, for example,

Major premise: All employees are classified as hourly or salaried
Minor premise: Alice is an employee who is not salaried
Conclusion: Alice is an hourly employee

Problems arise when the classifications are not dichotomous. Advertisers sometimes use invalid reasoning which becomes apparent when analyzed as a disjunctive syllogism. Such an ad may say something like this:

Why waste time collating photocopies? Get a Copymatic sorter. The implied premise is "Either you own a Copymatic sorter or you are wasting time collating." This reasoning is invalid if other efficient collating equipment is available to you.

The disjunctive syllogism fits in closely with our earlier discussion of either-or reasoning. Be wary of it. The classifications offered in the major premise must cover all possibilities.

A final type of syllogism is the *hypothetical* or *conditional syllogism*. This form is characterized by an "if" or "when" in its major premise.

Major premise: If the company cannot increase its share of the small car market, it will go out of business.
Minor premise: The company cannot increase its share of the small car market.
Conclusion: The company will go out of business.

The potential weak spot in a conditional syllogism is in the major premise's "if" or "when" statement. If it is not *unequivocably* true, the rest of the logic fails. Another flaw in reasoning arises when the minor premise (usually implied) contradicts the major premise. In the above example, if the minor premise says "the company *can* increase its share of the small car market" and the speaker concludes, "therefore the company *will be very profitable,*" the reasoning is invalid. The major premise says nothing about being very profitable.

Here's another example of a conditional syllogism using a "when" major premise.

Major Premise: When unemployment increases, inflation decreases.

Minor Premise: Unemployment is increasing.

Conclusion: Inflation will now decrease.

We need only look at recent economic history to see the fallacy in that argument!

Remember, there are cases where a logical deduction is *valid,* but the conclusion is still *wrong.* In such cases, the conclusion will be wrong because the premises (especially the major premise) are wrong. It's just another case of "garbage in, garbage out."

Communication professor Gary Cronkheit summarized a discussion of deductive reasoning aptly.

> I don't know who thinks in syllogisms or who carries rules for reasoning around in his head. But I do believe conscious attention to some of the ways communicators lead and mislead you can increase your awareness of the ways real-life messages are affecting you. Critical response to reasoning is difficult. It requires one to stop and think: What is really being said here?[10]

By looking critically at our own reasoning processes we can strengthen our communicative clout. Sound reasoning is at the heart of worthwhile messages. One more approach to reasoning and argument which, although not normally considered as a form of logic like induction and deduction, is the system based on the work of psychologist Dr. Carl R. Rogers. It is appropriately called the Rogerian approach.[11]

THE ROGERIAN APPROACH

Despite every effort to be reasonable and logical in presenting ideas to others, we sometimes find ourselves in situations where we feel helpless to convince the other person of our point of view. Ironically, such arguments often concern the issues about which we care most strongly—questions of principle, moral questions, personal loyalties. Too often communication breaks down because both parties are so emotionally involved, so deeply committed to certain values, that they can scarcely listen to each other, much less have a rational exchange of views. So we say, "There's no use arguing" or "You just can't reason with her" and give up.

Dr. Rogers, the noted authority on human relations, advises us not to admit defeat in dealing with such issues but instead to communicate to bring about understanding and change. Rogers points out that a chief impediment to personal communication is the tendency we all have to react to value statements with other value statements. If one of your employees remarks to you, "that new sales reps' compensation plan is lousy" your first impulse is

"In reply to Mr. Zimbalt's vicious attack on me I'd like to say that sticks and stones may break my bones but words from such a low-down, miserable little creep as Mr. Zimbalt will never harm me."

Carl Rogers suggests that communication problems can be avoided when we refrain from responding to value statements with other value statements.

probably not to ask him why he dislikes it, but to give your own opinion: "I think it's good" or "I agree." Almost inevitably, once two people have committed themselves to opposite stands on an issue, the possibility of their listening to a dissenting point of view with an open mind is sharply reduced. This would be especially true in the example cited if you had been instrumental in developing the compensation plan. Each goes on the defense, being more concerned with justifying his or her own opinion than with understanding the other person's point of view. The problem with throwing up such defensive barriers is compounded when we deal with issues that touch on our basic values. It is at this point that ordinary logical reasoning often quits. Hairston describes what happens:

> You can reason brilliantly or cajole in your most ingratiating tones, but the person whom you are addressing will not listen as long as you are presenting only your own side of the case. He *must* defend himself because you are threatening his values and thus his self-image. What can be done about such an impasse? Very little, if you are as unwilling as your audience is to yield or compromise. If, however, you are genuinely interested in solving the communication problem and coming to some kind of agreement, Rogers suggests that there is much you can do. You can begin by looking at the issue from the other person's point of view, that is, by trying to empathize with him. Real communication occurs, and this evaluative tendency is avoided, when we listen with understanding, What does it mean? It means *to see the expressed idea and attitude from the other person's point of view, to sense how it feels to him, to achieve his frame of reference in regard to the thing he is talking about.*[12]

Rogers suggests an experiment. When you find yourself in disagreement with others—and this applies to gathering data in your listener analysis preparation for your own presentation—try this approach. When someone says something you disagree with, give that person ample opportunity to express fully that disagreement. You can best do this by using what someone described as eloquent and encouraging grunts—"hum," "uh-huh," "oh," or "I see." When the person disagreeing pauses, simply continue to listen and nod thoughtfully until the person begins speaking again. Once the disagreement has been fully expressed you'll find that much of the emotion has gone out of it. Now you can begin to create understanding. Attempt to restate that person's ideas and feelings in your own words and then ask if that's what they mean. If not, try it again until you can restate their assertion in a way that is satisfactory to them. In doing so, you will find a more rational discussion emerging, differences being reduced, and those differences which remain becoming more understandable.

Obviously, this is a time-consuming and difficult approach to reasoning, and to undertake it you would have to care deeply about coming to an understanding with a person or group. When feelings are running high, however, the traditional kinds of argument are more apt to infuriate than convince an audience. Under such circumstances, a new approach at least is worth a try.[13]

The Rogerian approach offers real potential for reducing hostility and producing some degree of understanding and, perhaps agreement. But the approach is not an easy one. It requires a high degree of maturity and open-mindedness as well as a genuine interest in seeing the other person's point of view. As economist John Kenneth Galbraith said, "Faced with the choice between changing one's mind and proving that there is no need to do so, almost everyone gets busy on the proof."

Clearly, most people are uncomfortable making substantial changes in the ways they think. Changes involve certain risks. As Rogers points out: "If you really understand another person in this way, if you are willing to enter his private world and see the way life appears to him, without any attempt to make evaluative judgments, you run the risk of being changed yourself. You might see it his way, you might find yourself influenced in your attitudes or your personality."[14]

Although Roger's strategy for improving such communication was developed principally in a counseling context, it can readily be adapted to presentational speaking in business. An advantage the business speaker has (as compared to the public speaker) is that he or she can go to potential listeners and gather their opinions and feelings in the listener analysis stage of planning. By applying this technique, ideas can be more objectively worded to minimize the prospect of being tuned out by an irritated listener. It's certainly worth a try.

But remember, for this to work, you need to be more concerned with creating understanding than with winning an argument.

PREPARING YOUR MIND

Chapter 4. A summary of key ideas

1. Based on the work of Zelko and Dance, the concept of a "coping quotient" is discussed. The fewer irrelevant things we pay attention to, the more we can reduce speaker anxiety.
2. We can reduce anxiety-creating distractions by
    (a) preparing thoroughly,
    (b) being idea-conscious, not self-conscious, and
    (c) relaxing with a few deep breaths and a pause before beginning to talk.

3. Your listeners want you to succeed. A poor presentation can be just as uncomfortable for the audience as for the speaker.
4. Be sure you have something worth saying before preparing a presentation. Oral presentations can be an expense. Don't use a $100 medium to convey a 25¢ idea.
5. The ways we use language can be a major source of *mis*communication. Some common problems are:

    (a) failure to distinguish clearly between *facts* and *assumptions* or *inferences* (conclusions based on incomplete information). This problem can be overcome by a speaker using a "to me" clarifier to identify inferences.

    (b) failure to recognize that anything we say is a statement about ourselves. We make unique choices about words and their associations. Use of "to me" clarifiers can show that the speaker recognizes his word associations as personal interpretations.

    (c) use of oversimplified categories or polar terms which push observations into "black-white" without considering the many shades of gray. Such categories are seldom warranted and reflect upon the credibility of a speaker.

    (d) insensitivity to the way expectations are conveyed to others via our language. These tend to become self-fulfilling and can be counterproductive.

    (e) failure to recognize changes because we use relatively static words to describe dynamic processes.

    (f) failure to recognize that word meanings are in people, not the words themselves. Words are labels which trigger meanings. This triggering process is susceptible to individual interpretations in ways that make the conveying of absolutely accurate meaning difficult.

6. The business communicator has an obligation to be coherent and clear. Three approaches to reasoning suggest patterns for developing the fine art of thinking it through.
7. Inductive reasoning moves from observations or other evidence to a general conclusion. The most frequent pitfalls of this type reasoning are:

    (a) generalizing from too little evidence.

    (b) generalizing from poor quality or biased evidence, and

    (c) generalizing from irrelevant evidence.

8. Deductive reasoning takes generalizations and applies them to new situations. The logical form of argument called a syllogism provides a base for deduction. The validity of the deduction depends on the syllogism's ability to meet three criteria:

    (a) the premises must be true.

    (b) the major premise must include all cases.

      (c) the premises must be so related that they lead invariably to the conclusion.

9.   The Rogerian approach to reasoning attempts to overcome tendencies to react to the value statements of others with evaluations of our own. Such value statements tend to polarize points of view and hinder the creation of understanding.

10.   Rogers suggests that when we disagree with another's position, we should let the disagreement be fully expressed (even when rather emotional) and then attempt to restate that person's ideas and feelings in our own words. Then ask if that's what they mean. Keep rephrasing until agreement is reached on the wording. Doing this will remove the emotion from the issue, leaving the reasoning behind both parties' points of view open for logical analysis.

11.   The Rogerian approach can be especially useful in listener analysis data gathering. It can help the speaker more objectively word ideas to minimize the danger of "turning off" a listener.

NOTES

1.   Stephen S. Price. *Business Ideas: How to Create and Present Them.* (New York: Harper & Row Pub., 1967), p. 122.

2.   This discussion was adapted from Harold P. Zelko and Frank E. X. Dance, *Business and Professional Speech Communication,* 2nd ed. (New York: Holt, Rinehart and Winston, 1978), pp. 77–79.

3.   Ibid., p. 78.

4.   Some of the material in this section first appeared in Paul R. Timm, "The Way We Word," *Supervisory Management,* Vol. 23, No. 5, May 1978, pp. 20–26.

5.   George deMare. *Communicating for Leadership* (New York: Ronald Press Company, 1968), p. 224.

6.   Maxine Hairston. *A Contemporary Rhetoric* (Boston: Houghton-Mifflin Company, 1974), p. 180.

7.   Ibid., p. 189.

8.   J. Harold Janis. *Writing and Communicating in Business,* 3rd ed. (New York: Macmillan, 1978), p. 459.

9.   Ibid.

10.   Gary Cronkheit. *Communication and Awareness* (Menlo Park, Ca: Cummings Publishing Company, 1976), p. 251.

11.   Adapted from Hairston, op. cit., pp. 207–211.

12.   Hairston, p. 208.

13.   Ibid. p. 209.

14.   Carl R. Rogers, "Communication: Its Blocking and Facilitation," (Paper delivered at Northwestern University's Centennial Conference on Communication, October 11, 1951).

5

STATING AND SUPPORTING KEY IDEAS

OBJECTIVES OF CHAPTER 5

After studying this chapter, the reader should be able to:

1. Explain the three purposes of the statement of central theme.
2. Cite several examples of central theme statements for both informative and persuasive presentations.
3. Name and give examples of the four major dimensions of speaker credibility.
4. Name and give examples of seven specific types of support for key ideas available to the speaker.
5. Explain the difference between descriptive and inferential statistics with examples of each.

So far in this book we've put mind over matter. Before the contents of a presentation can be developed, proper mental attitude based on careful reasoning and listener analysis must be present. In Chapter 4 we discussed some principles of language use and reasoning in a general sense. Now it's time to apply these concepts to the specific presentation. So where do we begin? I'd suggest you first take a look at your *central theme* and *key ideas*.

YOUR CENTRAL THEME

Back in Chapter 2 we discussed preliminary planning using the TIMM's CAT memory aid. There we stressed the importance of clarifying your topic and intent. This planning forms the stuff from which your central theme will arise. The central theme is a summary statement of the entire presentation in capsule form. It is a carefully worded statement of what you intend to prove or demonstrate; it answers the underlying questions which were the catalyst for your presentation. Jean Michulka says that a statement of central theme should

1. Link the subject to your purpose and your audience.
2. State what you are going to talk about.
3. Express the idea in simple, precise words.[1]

The central theme determines the shape of the whole presentation. Take time to word your theme carefully, concisely, yet completely. Strip away irrelevant or tangential thoughts until you have a simple, clear statement. Here are some examples of central themes.

• A plant safety training class should be given to all first line supervisors.

• We should try a mail order sales approach for our new line of coaxial coordinators.

• My departmental budget must be increased by at least five percent to meet current work load.

• I want each employee to understand pension program eligibility and how benefit amounts can be calculated.

• The new sales compensation plan provides greater earning opportunities than ever if sales representatives focus on high profit items.

• Our new laser cloth-cutting machine is a smart buy for this company.

Once the central theme is specified, it becomes easier to distinguish key ideas which become the *bones* of your presentation.

Stating Your Key Ideas

Key ideas are the major thoughts, facts, or concepts that you want the audience to remember from your presentation. For example, let's build on the last central theme example cited. Say that you have been assigned to demonstrate persuasively your company's latest product, an expensive laser cloth-cutting machine, at a trade show for foreign garment manufacturers. Based on audience analysis, you know your listeners are dubious about purchasing this machine because it costs considerably more than competing equipment. You decide that the main points you want the audience to know are these:

1. The machine will cut more layers (thicknesses) of cloth than other machines used in the garment industry. It's more efficient.
2. Laser cutting does not snag knits and other delicate fabrics, as do other cutting methods.
3. The machine is lighter in weight and can be maneuvered to cut closer tolerances than other machines; there's less waste.
4. High reliability and simple design means that no expensive technicians are needed to operate or maintain the new laser cutter.

These are your key selling points. The remainder of your talk will build on these ideas. It's important to get these key ideas down on paper so you don't get sidetracked when developing the rest of the talk. At the end of this chapter is a Planning Worksheet on which key ideas may be listed. Another copy of this form is found in the book's appendix.

Here are some points to remember as you list the key ideas for your presentation:

1. State them as if they were conclusions to be drawn at the end of your presentation, preferably in complete sentences.
2. Be sure key ideas relate clearly to your overall main purpose such as getting agreement, convincing, or generating the desired action. In the preceding example, the key ideas all seek to persuade prospective customers to buy a laser cloth cutter.
3. State your ideas in specific terms so that they are thought provoking.
4. Use only a few key ideas. People have difficulty following more than four or five points. (Occasionally, your presentation has just one key idea. For example, a progress report may simply tell the audience "we are moving toward our goal on schedule" or "despite some unforeseen factors, we will still be able to meet our objectives.")

Once the bones of the presentation are provided via the key ideas, we can begin to fatten up the structure, building on these main points. Key ideas alone rarely convince an audience to accept or agree with your proposal. You must support, clarify, prove, or elaborate on the key ideas to get audience acceptance and/or action.

Let's take a look at some forms of support which will enhance the probability that your ideas will be accepted.

SUPPORTING YOUR KEY IDEAS

The first type of support I'll discuss is very general in that it permeates your entire presentation from the time you rise to speak (and maybe even before) until you conclude. Later I'll talk about some more specific techniques for supporting key points. First, the general one:

Your speaker credibility. One crucially important type of support for your assertion (which I'll touch upon here and come back to in other parts of this book) is your own *credibility*. This notion is as old as the ancient Greeks. Aristotle, in his treatise, *The Rhetoric*, explains that there are three types of arguments one may use to convince an audience: logical appeals *(logos)*, emotional appeals *(pathos)*, and ethical appeals *(ethos)*. "*Ethos*, according to tradition, is the most important of the three classical concepts."[2] In regard to ethos, Aristotle said: "There are three things which inspire confidence in the orator's own character—the three, namely, that induce us to believe a thing apart from any proof of it: good sense, good moral character, and good will. . . . There is no proof so effective as that of the character."[3]

"Will the meeting please come to order? Things are rocking along nicely. If there's no new business may I have a motion that the meeting be adjourned?"

Some oral presentations have only one key idea.

The term ethos has more recently been elaborated to refer to what we now call speaker *credibility*. Credibility is a kind of faith placed in you by others who perceive you as being intelligent, as having high standards, as being trustworthy, and so forth. It is cumulative and ongoing. What you say or do today will have a bearing on how others view your credibility tomorrow.

There has been considerable research into the concept of credibility. Some of these studies have sought to define what factors determine how others perceive our credibility. The findings suggest four primary dimensions of credibility:

1. *Expertise.* The degree to which you are informed about a particular topic affects your credibility. Generally, someone with high credibility has had training and/or experience relevant to the topic and is capable of displaying his or her competence. Citing respected sources of information and using illustrations which reflect upon your personal understanding of the topic helps convey such expertise.

2.   *Trustworthiness.* Credibility is enhanced when a speaker appears to be sincere and unbiased. You can create that impression by using facts and careful reasoning and by avoiding language that conveys emotionalism. Another technique that creates trust is to recognize and present opposing points of view. Such action shows that you are unbiased and not given to making hasty judgments. Finally, if you have no secret motives, such as personal gain, to be achieved from your talk your credibility may be strengthened. The salesman for TV advertising is likely to be less credible in an open discussion of the advantages of various ad media than, say, an individual who handles all types of advertising programs. A few years ago, the American Civil Liberties Union went to court to defend the rights of American Nazis to demonstrate. Many were surprised that the ACLU, which had more often been associated with "liberal" causes did this. But their credibility as an organization which will support the civil liberties of *anyone* was probably enhanced.

3.   *Composure.* Another factor affecting credibility is the degree of poise and confidence a speaker displays. The non-verbal factors such as appearance, posture, mannerisms, and facial expressions combine to create an impression for an audience. The speaker who is overly nervous, unorganized, or disheveled has low credibility. On the other hand, the speaker who is perfectly groomed, has practiced gestures, and makes a carefully choreographed presentation may arouse suspicion rather than trust. Most people prefer someone who looks his or her best and is positive, confident, spontaneous, and humble.

4.   *Dynamism.* Credibility is also affected by your personal dynamism: the tendency to be outgoing, friendly, and articulate. A shy, apprehensive person often appears less credible than his more extroverted counterpart. However, we again suggest moderation; the loudmouthed, totally uninhibited charater may be dynamic but not very credible.

To summarize, credibility involves more than superficial qualities, it is a combination of the past image you've created and present impressions you are making. You can't erase the past, but you can strive to enhance your credibility today by conveying a sense of expertise (by being *thoroughly* prepared), trustworthiness (by being scrupulously fair and *above board* in your arguments and your motives), composed (by being *polished* in your presentation), and dynamic (by sharing your genuine *enthusiasm* for what you're saying).

Incidentally, of these dimensions of credibility, *trustworthiness* has repeatedly been shown to be the most important.

Specific support for key ideas. As I said earlier in this chapter, credibility is a general form of support which permeates your entire presentation. Now let's look at several specific forms of support for key ideas.

Details or explanations of each key idea is a common kind of support; however, it is not necessarily the most effective. This type of support simply restates or explains in different words what the key idea asserts. Such support may be prefaced by remarks such as "Let me explain why I've said that" or "Another way to say this might be . . ." and so forth. From my experience, most people rely too heavily on this type of support when other, more interesting ways could be used. Try, instead, to work on some other techniques such as the following:

Comparisons or analogies often provide excellent support. An apt analogy can communicate a concept or idea far more clearly and interestingly than a mere explanation can. Often analogies are short narratives such as the one I overheard at a convention: A young professor asked an older, established author how long it had taken to complete his most recent book. Instead of giving a lengthy explanation, the elder man used an analogy from his own life: "I was a soldier on leave in Paris just after the war in 1945, and I stopped to watch a sidewalk artist painting. When I asked if one painting was for sale, the artist said yes and quoted me the price. I exclaimed, 'But it only took you an hour to paint that!' The indignant artist replied, 'But I have been preparing all my life!' "

The author made his point perfectly clear with an analogy, and the younger man learned a valuable lesson while hearing an interesting story. Analogies or comparisons can be commanding in a presentation. However, remember that the comparison must be apt: The things compared must be alike in nearly all respects.

Examples, especially those from your personal experience, are good sources of support for key ideas; they also give credibility to you as a speaker. If you choose this method of support, be sure that your experience is not an isolated case but rather is exemplary of a general condition of the key idea. For example, let's say the key idea is, "Lower wages and salaries at our plant are a cause of high labor turnover." Reporting a discussion about low pay with one or even two disgruntled employees wouldn't be sufficient evidence to support the key idea. If, however, you can put together several such experiences, your support will be much stronger. It might sound like this:

Key idea: Lower wages and salaries here are a cause of higher labor turnover.
Supporting examples:

- Three first line supervisors in three different departments have left the company during the past month to work for another company paying higher wages.

- Fifty-three percent of our employees—most right out of high school—stay with us only nine months or less. Our training program for most skilled jobs is three months. It appears that once they have some experience, these young people leave us for better paying jobs elsewhere.

• Two supervisors have reported that employees in their work groups have been talking about contacting the labor relations board office to try to get a union election held.

Such a series of examples provide inductive support to the key idea. This line of reasoning is logically sound and likely to be convincing.

Definitions are sometimes useful to support key ideas by clarifying specialized terms your listeners may not know. Put these into your own words rather than read from a dictionary—and be careful not to talk down to your audience. You might say something like "Many of you are no doubt familiar with semiconductor technology but let me review quickly what I mean for those who aren't."

Avoid using a dictionary definition as a major point. "Webster's defines xxx as . . . blah, blah, etc." is a real turn-off to many listeners. Often a humorous definition can be effective at holding attention and making a point. "Diplomacy has been defined as the art of letting someone else have your way" is catchy and could well support a key idea.

Taking a moment to define a term which may be unfamiliar insures that your audience can stay with you. Often listeners will not risk embarrassment by asking you to define a term; you should take the initiative to clarify. Author Ralph Woods gives an example:

"Of course, no doubt most everyone here knows what the inside of a corpuscle is like," said the lecturer on health. "Most of us do," interrupted the chairman, "but for the benefit of those who have never been inside one, you had better explain it."

Use definitions sparingly unless you are covering a whole new area for the listener. Then, put definitions in your own words whenever possible.

Statistics provide another means of supporting a key idea. Mark Twain's oft quoted line, "There are liars and there are damn liars; and then there are statistics" points out a potential problem. You no doubt know ways in which statistics can be used to distort information, but any form of "lying with statistics" is a poor choice and will eventually cause a gap in your credibility. Be comfortable with the statistics and their implications before you use them. Understand how statistics are derived and how to interpret them. Generally, there are two kinds of statistics: descriptive and inferential. *Descriptive statistics* take a large quantity of numbers and make another, smaller set of numbers out of the data while retaining the essential information. In short, they condense or describe the large body of data in terms more understandable to an audience. Often this information is displayed as graphs, charts, or pictograms. *Inferential statistics* are mathematical probabilities that a given conclusion is true, based on evidence provided by sampling. For example, if X is true for 1000 people who were questioned at random in a midwestern city, then X will probably be true for any segment of the population in that city. Inferential statistics apply to the science of making decisions in the face of uncertainty; deciding on the basis of incomplete information.

Before you decide what kind of statistics to use in your presentation, consider your audience's ability to understand statistical information. Most people have little trouble with descriptive statistics, but inferential statistics frequently confuse. If you decide to use statistics, these guidelines help you use them more effectively.

1. Round off large numbers so they are more easily grasped.
2. Interpret the numbers so they are meaningful to the listener. Percentages can be understood by most people.
3. Use statistics sparingly. Anything used to excess becomes commonplace or boring.
4. Be sure to compare "apples to apples." I recently heard a speaker express relief that our unemployment rate was only six or seven percent. In Israel, she exclaimed, "One person in 18 is unemployed!" That, of course, is virtually the same percentage.

As I said a moment ago, most people can readily grasp descriptive statistics but are rather confused by probabilities. Here's a personal example. I recently heard a speaker misusing actuarial data, a very complex form of inferential statistics, compiled by an insurance company to project life span based on health habits. He told his audience such things as "If you smoke more than 2 packs of cigarettes a day, subtract 8 years from your life, if you walk 3 miles a day, add 7 years, etc." By the time he finished, half of his audience figured they'd live forever, and the other half wondered why they weren't already dead. The point is that the speaker didn't understand these actuarial data and he conveyed this lack of understanding only too clearly to his listeners.

The *Formal Quotation* is less frequently used in business briefings than in public speeches. But it can be effective if we choose to quote an authority who is

1. Recognized as an expert by your listeners
2. In a position to know about the specific point you are trying to support
3. In general agreement with other authorities on the subject
4. Free from prejudice which would distort his or her view.

The person you quote doesn't have to be a national or international figure. It may be someone in your own organization who has had a lot of training or experience and whose ideas and name would be recognized and valued by your listeners.

When deciding whether or not a person you intend to quote is free from prejudice or self-interest, ask yourself, "What does he or she have to gain from making such a statement?" If it is apparent that the authority has only his or her best interests at heart, your source will not be credible.

Audio-visual supports are becoming more important because many people in any given audience have grown up in a "television age" and are conditioned to visual as well as aural messages. Visuals can be used in conjunction with any kind of support to enhance your presentation. In Chapter 9 we'll discuss the use of such materials.

Support from your listeners is one other technique that should be used whenever possible. Here, you get the listeners to participate in making your case by having them provide information. Let's say, for example, that your talk is stressing the need for additional security equipment in a retail store, and your audience includes several store managers. Instead of quoting statistics, you might ask the store managers specific questions—preferably ones they're likely to know the answers to! "Margaret, how much has your store lost to shoplifters this year?" or, "How do these losses compare to last year?" Be sure that you have the information in case Margaret can't recall off hand. And be careful not to embarrass her if she doesn't know.

Getting such support "from the horse's mouth" can be effective in illustrating your point.

Getting It Down on Paper

The worksheet presented in Figure 5-1 provides a simple way to assemble the skeleton of a talk: the central theme and key ideas. Another copy of this form appears in the Appendix.

Having identified your main points and developed support for each, you are now ready to organize the presentation. In Chapter 6 we'll discuss patterns of organization that can give power to your presentations.

STATING AND SUPPORTING KEY IDEAS

Chapter 5. A summary of key ideas.

1. The statement of central theme serves to
    (a) link your subject to your purpose and your audience,
    (b) state what you are going to talk about, and
    (c) express the heart of your message in concise terms.
2. The central theme plus key idea statements provide the "bones" around which the presentation is built.

FIGURE 5-1
Identifying central theme, key ideas, and forms of support (worksheet)

1. Purpose: What are your objectives for this presentation? State them in terms of the *specific attitude change* or *course of action* you hope to bring about in the audience.

2. State your central theme clearly and concisely. (Be sure it meets the criteria suggested in this chapter.)

3. First list the key ideas you want your audience to understand. Next list the specific support information you will use for each key idea.
   Key Idea A
   Support Information

   Key Idea B
   Support Information

   Key Idea C
   Support Information

   Key Idea D
   Support Information

   Key Idea E
   Support Information

4. How will you attempt to project high credibility? Be specific.

3. Speaker credibility is a general form of key idea support which permeates the entire presentation. The four dimensions of ethos or speaker credibility are

    (a) expertise with regard to the topic of the talk
    (b) trustworthiness
    (c) composure, and
    (d) dynamism.

4. Specific forms of support for key ideas include

    (a) details or explanations
    (b) comparison or analogies
    (c) examples
    (d) definitions
    (e) statistics
    (f) formal quotations
    (g) audio-visual support
    (h) listener participation.

NOTES

1. Jean H. Michulka. *Let's Talk Business* (Cincinnati: South-Western Publishing Co., 1978), p. 284.
2. Elwood Murray, Gerald M. Phillips and J. David Truby. *Speech: Science Art* (Indianapolis: Bobbs-Merrill, 1969), p. 29.
3. Aristotle, *Rhetoric,* $1377_b21-1378_a19$.
4. Ralph L. Woods. *The Modern Handbook of Humor* (New York: McGraw-Hill, 1967), p. 449.

6

ARRANGING IDEAS FOR CLARITY AND IMPACT

OBJECTIVES OF CHAPTER 6

After studying this chapter, the reader should be able to:

1. Name and describe the five principles of outlining.
2. Describe a common symbolization pattern for outlines.
3. Explain when direct ("big idea first") and indirect ("big idea later") patterns of arrangement are most appropriate.
4. Name and give examples of the seven patterns of arrangement (in addition to direct and indirect).
5. Explain several techniques for making your main points stand out to your listeners.

To develop clarity and impact in a talk, we need to arrange the main and supporting ideas in a meaningful way to show their relationship to the central theme and to each other. This organizing process will affect how clearly we are understood, how well our thoughts will be remembered, and what the audience thinks of us. A message without systematic flow is likely to sound like the story in the Broom Hilda cartoon on page 85. Let me suggest the age old notion of outlining as the only way I know to insure a coherent message.

PRINCIPLES OF OUTLINING

An outline is a crucially important working tool. It categorizes information and separates main ideas from subordinate ones. All forms of outlining share certain basic principles. These principles include simplicity, coordination, subordination, progression, and symbolization.[1]

Simplicity. The outline as a message-organizing tool should assist, not confuse its user. Each line of it should represent a single bit of information. This information may be written out in a full sentence, but more often, a phrase or key word is more useful. Full sentence outlines are often too cumbersome. Use the old KISS principle: "Keep it simple, speakers."

Coordination. The principle of coordination means that all points within subdivision (and ultimately within the whole talk) must be logically related. For example, let's say your talk is to explain the new sales representative's compensation plan. You've decided to cover these main points

Chicago Tribune-New York News Syndicate, Inc.

A message without sequence will lose your listener.

1982 Sales Representatives' Compensation Program
I.   Special Incentives
    A. Deluxe model machine bonus of $200
    B. Extra points awarded to sales reps over 150% of plan
    C. Gift award to top sales rep each month
    D. Penalty for failure to turn in orders within 24 hours is forfeiture of
       all bonus compensation

As you look at each item under "special incentives" you'll note that entry D is out of place. Item D does not offer a postive incentive to sell more but rather warns the representative to get paper work in on time to avoid forfeiting compensation. This item should be placed elsewhere in the talk, under another category.

Subordination. The principle of subordination refers to the way a main idea is divided into subordinate parts. Each entry in the outline should relate directly to the preceding category. In the example, "Special Incentives" relates directly to the overall theme, "1982 Sales Representatives' Compensation Plan." Similarly, items A, B, and C are subordinate in that they describe specific types of special incentives.

Progression. The parts of a talk must be arranged in some logical pattern to show progression from point to point. The remainder of this chapter illustrates orders of arrangement which may be used. More than one pattern may be used within a given talk, but be sure to stay consistent within that pattern. For example, the key ideas (main headings) may fit into a chronological arrangement but subpoints under a main heading may use a cause and effect pattern for clarity.

Symbolization. Symbolization is the way you denote the coordination, subordination, and progression of a talk. Typically we use a combination of Roman numbers, Arabic numbers, capital letters and lower case letters. If any heading is to be subdivided, several subheadings should follow. For example, point A should be followed by at least numbers 1 and 2. The most common symbolization pattern for outlines is illustrated in Figure 6-1.

FIGURE 6-1
A common system of symbols for arranging an outline

1. FIRST LEVEL HEADINGS
    A. Second level headings
        1. Third level headings
            a. Fourth level headings
                (1) Fifth level headings
                  (a) Sixth level headings

Developing an outline forces one to clarify key points and put them into a systematic format. The remainder of this chapter looks at some commonly used patterns of arrangement. We often use a combination of several of these.

A DIRECT PATTERN: "BIG IDEA" FIRST

This method presents the *main idea* or your *conclusion* FIRST. That idea is then developed by presenting supporting information. This kind of organization uses *deductive logic,* that is, a general statement followed by supporting information. For some reason, many people resist this approach. They perhaps fancy themselves as an Agatha Christie or Alfred Hitchcock, popping a surprise conclusion on their audience. Although mysteries can be entertaining, most people in business don't like to be surprised. They want to know what you're driving at. So try starting with your *big idea.* Here is an example:

(Major Theme) Buying a duplex for income property is a good investment.

I.   (Big Idea) 20.2% RETURN AVAILABLE FROM A SAFE INVESTMENT
    A. $1010 net return per year on an investment of only $5,000
    B.   The same $5,000 would earn only $300 in a bank
    C.   This investment is secure and provides tax advantages
II. THIS BUILDING WILL EARN MONEY FOR YOU
    A.   Renovated building will gross at least $3,600 per year in rents
        1. Apartment 1 rents for $140 per month
        2. Apartment 2 rents for $160 per month
    B.   Owner's expenses are about $2,590 per year

1. Property tax	$ 400
2. Insurance	$ 100
3. Mortgage payments	$1,440
4. Depreciation	$ 640

    C.   Many of these costs are tax deductible
    D.   Buildings in this neighborhood are appreciating at a rate of approximately 10 percent per year
III. YOUR INVESTMENT IS SECURE
    A.   Closeness to the University assures occupancy
        1. Over past 5 years, both apartments have been occupied year-round
        2. Expansion of size of university insures demand
    B.   Utility rate increases will not affect earnings since tenants pay own
IV. HOW TO TAKE ADVANTAGE OF THIS INVESTMENT
    A. $3,000 down payment to purchase
        1. Conventional mortgage can be assumed
        2. 9½% interest rate
    B. $2,000 needed for repairs
        1. Painting, gutters and exterior repairs

2. New water heater, Apt. #1
3. Replace commode, sink, Apt. #2
4. Miscellaneous cleanup

The direct order gets to the point first and then explains the details. If you organized this talk saving the big idea (20.2 percent return on investment) for last, you'd run several risks, (1) your audience may be lead to expect a greater return and would be disappointed at what they may see as a modest 20.2 percent, or (2) the supporting detail would be confusing since the point (main idea) being supported isn't clear until the very end by which time they've forgotten half of what you said. It's easier for us to remember evidence if we know what it's supporting.

Many, in fact *most,* business presentations can, and should, use a direct approach. It's efficient, logical, and business-like. Remember to lead with your "ace"—the big idea—and then provide the necessary support.

There are, however, at least two cases where the direct approach is less appropriate. These are when (1) your listener is likely to oppose the ideas you are advocating, and (2) background information is needed before your listener

Reprinted by permission

"Gentlemen, I have good news and bad news."

Your opening remarks should get straight to the point when you use a direct order of arrangement. . . .

can understand your main point. An alternative plan of organization which could be used in such cases is the indirect pattern.

INDIRECT PATTERN: "BIG IDEA" LATER

The indirect method which uses *inductive logic,* presents the supporting details first and the main point later. The outline below shows how the indirect plan may be used. Assume that the audience is not very excited about the speaker's purpose which is to implement a hospital care audit program

I. WHAT ARE WE CURRENTLY DOING TO EVALUATE OUR HOSPITAL?
    A. Several unstructured data gathering attempts by individual administrators
    B. No formal program

II. WHAT ARE THE OTHER INSTITUTIONS DOING TO EVALUATE?
    A. Utilization Review
    B. Patient Care Audit

III. WHAT IS UTILIZATION REVIEW?
    A. Mandated by Social Security Act of 1965 (initiated Medicare/Medicaid)
    B. Purpose: To assure the government that services for which it is paying are appropriate and cost-effective
    C. How it Works

IV. WHAT IS PATIENT CARE AUDIT?
    A. Mechanics of
    B. Advantages of
        1. Provides systematic documentation of problems
        2. Provides in-service education to implement corrective action
        3. Participation in audit improves staff morale
        4. Finds strong points and identifies those areas that need improving

V. WHY SHOULD NEWHOUSE MEASURE THE QUALITY OF PATIENT CARE?
    A. To meet federal government regulations for Medicare/Medicaid services
    B. To meet hospital goal of professional certification for a psychiatric facility
    C. To increase professionalism

Key Idea
VI.   WHAT IF WE DON'T ACCEPT THIS CHALLENGE TO MEASURE
      THE QUALITY OF SERVICES?
      A.   Continued uncertainty about our quality of care
      B.   Government regulators will step in and do it for us
Main Idea
VII. PATIENT CARE AT NEWHOUSE STATE HOSPITAL CAN BEST
      BE MEASURED BY A UTILIZATION REVIEW AND A PATIENT
      CARE AUDIT PROGRAM

This method of organization builds from lesser ideas to your most forceful ammunition (i.e., "government regulators will do it for us"). For that reason, this method often works for persuasive presentations in which you don't want to come on too strong at first, causing the audience to tune you out before you have a chance to convince them.

The direct and indirect patterns are the two general approaches to organizing. Within these, there are a variety of ways to arrange ideas in a systematic way. Descriptions of several of these patterns of arrangement follow.

CHRONOLOGICAL ORDER PATTERN

With the chronological method of organization, we arrange key ideas as they occur in time. The approach is especially useful when instructing someone on step-by-step procedures or when giving a progress report. The pattern has an important advantage: It is predictable. That helps listeners follow—where you've been and where you're going. Of course, this predictability can be a disadvantage if it is overused. Sometimes we opt for a chronological pattern when other approaches would be more interesting. Some excellent history books avoid the traditional chronological arrangement and instead deal with historical themes or issues, an approach that makes them more interesting.

A reverse chronological order, going from the recent to the past, also adds variety. In short, chronological arrangement can be useful in cases where your listeners need to understand the development of your ideas over time.

CRITERIA-APPLICATION PATTERN

This pattern can be a very effective approach in presentations which offer solutions to problems. Early in the presentation, criteria or standards for evaluation are suggested. Then, possible solutions or choices are compared against those standards. This approach illuminates your underlying reasoning and can be very convincing so long as the audience agrees with your decision criteria. (Getting them to say they agree before you offer the big idea helps.)

Let's say, for example, that you are advocating the purchase of a particular make of truck for your company fleet. You might establish these major criteria early in the talk:

The trucks we purchase must:

1. Be capable of carrying our normal loads.
2. Be fuel efficient (at least 14 mpg)
3. Be serviced locally by reputable dealers
4. Cost less than $12,000 each

We would then discuss several makes of trucks to see how well each meets our criteria. Minor or secondary criteria should similarly be developed. The conclusion simply recommends the truck that best meets the agreed upon criteria.

When using this approach, be sure to spell out in as much detail as possible the specific decision criteria. These should describe the best possible case or the ideal. Then see which of the available alternatives comes closest to meeting the ideal.

CAUSE-EFFECT PATTERN

This approach can be used to explain how something occurred (how we got into this "fine kettle of fish" as Laurel and Hardy would have said), or to predict the consequences of some action. Although this pattern seems simple, it can be tricky. The problem arises when we confuse the causes and the effects. An example of this cause-effect confusion has emerged in management studies. In recent years we've seen increasing examples of relationships between work environment and productivity. From this, many people conclude that a happy worker is a productive worker. But is it the happiness that makes him productive, or the productiveness that makes him happy? Causality is not always clear.

If there is anything we've learned through the ecology movement of the past decade or so, it is that causes and effects are a lot more complicated than they may appear. Often effects are unforeseen (Who would have anticipated damage to the ozone from aerosol sprays?) and causes baffling.

If you use this pattern of arrangement, be cautious to substantiate the causal relationship. Don't just assume that because two phenomena occur in sequence that one causes the other. On the other hand, don't be overly optimistic about results of actions. "If only we had a training program for supervisors, we wouldn't have all these morale problems." Nothing is quite that simple—or certain.

PROBLEM-SOLUTION PATTERN

The problem-solution method of organization requires you to give much time and effort to clarifying or making your audience aware of a problem or a need. Once the listener feels the problem is significant to him or her personally, *voila*—you introduce your solution. Your listeners will then accept your proposal, anxious to alleviate this felt need. At least that's the way it's supposed to work! Figure 6-2 describes this persuasive model.

Much TV advertising uses this method of organizing its message.* For example, we watch someone shaving and suddenly they get nicked by the razor: *(the problem)*. We remember how many times *we* have had the same thing happen to us: *(personalizing the problem)*. Then we are told that a new razor is designed to "float" over the skin surface, never nicking us: *(the solution)*. A few seconds later the miracle of television takes us into an old fashioned living room (like Mom's and Dad's) where a man is being encouraged to stuff himself at the dinner table by an overweight lady (like Mom?) resulting in a stomach disorder. The solution: "plop, plop; fizz, fizz."

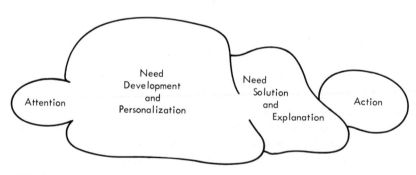

FIGURE 6-2
A problem-solution persuasive model

---

*TV commercials are, of course, more abbreviated than business presentations. Still, the persuasive pattern used is interesting to observe.

Let's look at an example of how this problem-solution approach might work in a brief, business-related presentation. The facts are:

Problem:	In the past six months our use of long distance telephone calls has increased by 70% but there has been no decrease in our use of letters and teletype. Right now, our phone bills exceed $850 per month. At that rate, we will be spending $10,200 a year for long distance calls. For that amount, we could hire another desperately-needed clerical employee.
Need Development:	Even though this large increase in phone expenses is alarming, the idea that these costs are not going to decrease really bothers me. Without better control of this expense, our profit will
Personalizing:	decline and ultimately *our individual earnings* will suffer. We and our company cannot continue to prosper with such expenses.
Solution:	I believe there is a way to deal with this problem. A phone company representative has discussed the possibility of installing a WATS line. These are some cost figures . . .
Action:	I'd like your approval to order WATS line service.

The problem-solution pattern of arrangement is best suited for persuasive presentations. The keys to its effectiveness lie in (1) *personalizing the problem* so that your audience really *feels the need* to do something about it, (2) showing them in unequivocal terms that *your* proposed *solution will in fact solve the problem,* and (3) giving them some specific *action they can take* to bring about this desired solution. It is helpful to make the recommended action as easy for them as possible. We'll talk more about this persuasive pattern in Chapter 11.

TOPICAL OR SPATIAL ORDER PATTERN

The topical order plan will work for presentations dealing with different but related ideas. The topics or examples should be arranged so each one logically reinforces the preceding one. For example, a talk about cost-cutting may stress an overall theme of economizing and then reinforce that theme by stressing certain areas such as:

- recycling waste in the shop
- cutting postage and mailing costs
- reducing use of company vehicles

The space order may cite support for the theme by organizing key ideas from far away to close by or vice versa. For example, we might report on our bank's building and remodeling program by describing progress on (1) a new, outlying office, (2) the addition to the midtown branch, and (3) remodeling of the teller facilities at the main office. This is a simple pattern but one that gives coherence to your talk.

INCREASING MAGNITUDE OR DIFFICULTY PATTERN

A briefing on the effects of the economy on business may develop from relatively local, temporary factors to the more complex, national, or worldwide trends. For example, a slowdown in sales in a downtown shoe store may be attributed to

- increasing competition from stores in outlying shopping malls.
- a temporary layoff at the town's major factory.
- delays in getting high-demand shoes from distributors.
- worldwide shortages of quality leather.

Each of these points represents increasing difficulty for the local businessman. He may be able to do something about the first point and even the second (for example, extend credit to workers temporarily out of a job), but the third and fourth become more difficult to cope with. This order of arrangement is also good for instructing listeners. To teach, a speaker begins with something familiar or already known by the listener and moves to the unknown or more complex. For example, training on the use of a new machine could begin by first reviewing the operation of a machine your listeners are already familiar with, and then proceeding to point out these basic similarities in using the unfamiliar new machine.

ORDER OF IMPORTANCE PATTERN

Particularly useful in the progress report, this arrangement presents the most significant or noteworthy point first with other developments following in descending order of importance. For example, main ideas may be

1. The wind tunnel tests of the missile tail assembly were successful.
2. The electronic malfunction problem in the sensing device has been narrowed down to two possible causes.

3.   The engineers are considering the use of a different coating which will be more resistant to tear.

Often you will use a combination of several of these patterns of arrangement in a talk. Figure 6-3 shows how this might be done for a technical presentation.[2]
To help you remember better the various methods of organization discussed in this chapter and what type of presentation each is most useful for, Figure 6-4 summarizes the methods we've discussed.

MAKE SURE YOUR MAIN POINTS STAND OUT

A careful and appropriate arrangement of your key ideas goes a long way toward helping your listeners get the gist of your message. If you have organized carefully, the main ideas and central theme will all fit together and make sense. The more obvious your organizational structure is to your audience, the more power it can add to your presentation.

In written reports, writers can identify main ideas by using different typefaces, underlining, and by placing headings and subheadings in an orderly fashion. Readers come to recognize different levels of headings as having different degrees of importance.

In oral presentations you can use most of these same techniques, though in a slightly different form. Instead of a table of contents or series of headings and subheadings, you can use a chart or overhead transparency to preview main points you will cover. Or, in less formal occasions, you could write out your key points on a transparency or chalk-board as you speak. We'll discuss visual aids in more detail in Chapter 9.

Regardless of whether you use aids or not, you must highlight your key points. To do so, Roger Wilcox says, ". . . it is absolutely essential that you make generous use of previews, transitions, and summaries (both internal and final)."[3] Frequently remind your listeners of what you've just covered and where you are going from here. It may sound repetitious to you, but remember that your listeners are not as familiar with the talk as you are and repetition is a way to help them understand. Unlike a written report, an oral presentation doesn't permit your message receivers to flip back through the pages to clarify the structure in their minds. It's your job to help them do that. Previews, summaries and transitions together may need to make up as much as 25 percent of the total presentation.

Again quoting Wilcox: "Thus, whether visually or verbally—or both—you must make certain the listener understands clearly your topic or title, your specific purpose, your plan of development, the main headings and

FIGURE 6-3
Combining patterns of arrangement

RAPIDLY MACHINE-DRILL PARTS FOR STORAGE AT ASSEMBLY POINT

- I. Elements of machine drilling
    - A. Get part to work table
        1. secure part
        2. secure work table
    - B. Control work table ── Chronological Pattern
        1. one-axis movement ┐
        2. two-axis movement ├ Spatial or Topical Pattern
        3. three-axis movement ┘
    - C. Test part
    - D. Remove part
        1. extraction ┐
        2. moving ├ Smaller Chronological Pattern
        3. storage ┘
- II. Present Methods
    - A. Hand operation
        1. disadvantages
            a. slow
            b. dangerous ── Topical with Sub-patterns of Cause-Effect
            c. inaccurate
            d. costly
    - B. Partial automatic control
        1. disadvantages
            a. wastes material
            b. unutilized operator time

A NEW SYSTEM FOR FULLY CONTROLLED AUTOMATIC PRECISION DRILLING

- I. Combined two-phased operation
    - A. Automatic conveyor moves part to table
        1. special attachment secures part
            a. simultaneously securing table
    - B. Tape unit permits variable axis control ── Chronological Pattern ── Cause to Effect Pattern
    - C. Depth and diameter control eliminates testing
    - D. Conveyor access transport
        1. removes
        2. conveys
        3. packages
- II. Advantages
    - A. Load time reduced 50%
    - B. Operator danger removed
    - C. Errors reduced to 0.002%
    - D. Cost reduced ── Effect to Cause Pattern
        1. no waste
        2. one operator per two machines
    - E. Compatible with future developments

Source: Printed by permission of John Wiley & Sons, Inc., Publishers.

Figure 6-4
Arranging main points in a presentation

Kind of Presentation	Purpose of Presentation	Recommended Methods of Organization for Body of Presentation
Persuasive	1. Get audience to accept ideas or 2. Get audience to do something ("sell" them)	1. *Inductive Pattern:* Show several specific examples, lines of reasoning, which lead to a general conclusion or action. 2. *Problem-Solution Pattern:* Describe a problem vividly to create a "need" for a solution; then offer audience your solution to the problem. 3. *Criteria-Application Pattern:* Describe criteria which pose an ideal or "best possible case." Then compare alternatives against these. Your recommended solution is the one that fits best.
Informational	Inform the audience (teach them something)	1. *Deductive Pattern:* Present the conclusion first and then explain the details which support such a conclusion. 2. *Chronological Pattern:* Show how several events developed over a period of time. 3. *Topical or Spatial Pattern:* a) Give several examples which relate to your topic. b) Give examples from different places, relating to the topic. 4. *Increasing Difficulty Pattern:* Start with something known to the audience; then add more complex or unusual concepts. 5. *Chain of Events Pattern:* Show how a series of steps or procedures lead to your conclusion.
Progress Report	Inform or update knowledge of a familiar subject	1. *Chronological Pattern:* (as discussed above) 2. *Deductive Pattern:* (as discussed above) 3. *Order of Importance Pattern:* Start with most significant finding and arrange others in descending order or vice-versa.

subheadings for any section or subsection of your discussion, and your final conclusions. The *structure* of your talk must be unmistakably clear. Remember, your listener wants to see ahead where you are going, know where you are at any given point, and understand what conclusions you read in the end. He or she does not like to feel lost."[4]

The effective arrangement of clearly stated and adequately substantiated key ideas is crucial to effective oral presentations. Take time to think through your patterns of organization.

"Before we head into the annual meeting, gentlemen, I thought a quick little review of just who we are might be in order."

Your listeners don't like to feel lost

Source: From *Good News, Bad News* by Henry Martin. Copyright © 1969, 1970, 1971, 1972, 1973, 1974, 1975, 1976, 1977 Henry R. Martin. Used by permission of Charles Scribner's Sons.

ARRANGING IDEAS FOR CLARITY
AND IMPACT

Chapter 6. A summary of key ideas

1. Arrangement of key ideas will have an effect on how clearly we are understood, how well our listeners will remember what we've said, and what our audience thinks of us.
2. Effective outlines illustrate the characteristics of simplicity, coordination, subordination, and progression.
3. A "big idea first" pattern of arrangement is often best for business presentations.
4. A "big idea later" pattern of arrangement is preferred when you anticipate audience resistance to a proposal or when you must present background information before a conclusion can be understood.
5. Ideas may be arranged according to
   (a) chronological order
   (b) criteria-application
   (c) cause-effect
   (d) problem-solution
   (e) topical or spatial order
   (f) increasing magnitude or difficulty, or
   (g) order of importance.
6. Often a combination of several patterns is used in a talk.
7. It is important to help your listener visualize your patterns of arrangement by verbally clarifying and/or using visual aids.

NOTES

1. Adapted from Glen E. Mills, *Putting a Message Together* (Indianapolis: Bobbs-Merrill, 1972), pp. 26–29.
2. W.A. Mambert, *Presenting Technical Ideas* (New York: John Wiley Inc., 1968), pp. 192–193. Reprinted by permission of John Wiley & Sons, Inc., Publishers.
3. Roger P. Wilcox, *Communication at Work* (Boston: Houghton Mifflin Company, 1977), pp. 465–6.
4. Ibid., p. 466.

7

BEGINNINGS, TRANSITION, AND ENDINGS:
the ties that bind

OBJECTIVES OF CHAPTER 7

After studying this chapter, the reader should be able to:

1. Name several nonverbal ways we communicate even before we get up to give a talk.
2. Explain the three major purposes of the introduction as well as three additional functions it may serve.
3. Describe how listener expectations can be created using the classroom game discussed in this chapter.
4. Name and develop an original example of the six techniques for introducing a talk discussed in this chapter.
5. Describe five "sure-fire ways to flop" in your introduction.
6. Explain the function of transitions.
7. Name four things which should have been accomplished as you end a presentation.

In any communication situation, your listeners will have a set of *a priori* assumptions about what you're going to say or do. These expectations come from their perceptions of you, your roles or position, your appearance, their past experiences with people "of your type," and a myriad of other subtle and often illogical cues. Sometimes these expectations work for you; your reputation for creativity and your ability to solve problems precedes you, giving a "halo effect." In other cases you may need to overcome some negative assumptions and win over your listeners. Your listener analysis should provide clues as to how you're likely to be received, but you can't always be sure. The safest approach is to assume that you'll need to win over at least some of your listeners early in the talk. This is one of the key functions of your introductory remarks: to bind your listeners to you. This is the beginning of the creation of understanding. But even before your introduction, you are conveying subtle messages to others.

WE COMMUNICATE BEFORE WE BEGIN TO TALK

We need to keep in mind that communication, that is, the way we project "cues" to other individuals, is not something we can turn on and off at will. If

102

you are scheduled to give a briefing or presentation, people are likely to be observing your actions even before you get up to speak. As one author puts it, "Your manner in waiting to give your speech is as important as your material or your presentation."[1]

When people know that you are going to give a talk, they begin to observe you and draw some conclusions about you from your behaviors. If you or the topic you are going to be talking about is of particular interest to them they are likely to look you over pretty carefully. Some speakers seem to be totally oblivious to this. Preston gives an example of such people:

"During the program they may bury their heads in the speech they're going to make. Or they may simply sit like a bump on a log, looking bored, tense, or grim, and not uttering a word to anyone on either side. Then he or she is introduced. Bounding up, he or she is suddenly Mr. or Ms. charm."

"Mr. Sloane, the directors are seated in the conference room waiting for you to make your grand entrance with humble apologies for keeping them waiting."

We start to communicate even before we begin our presentation. Anything we do (or don't do) can convey meaning to our listeners.

"Unfortunately, if you don't look the part before, the audience won't buy that. Even humor won't turn on an audience already turned off by the speaker's actions. What you do on stage—and the speaker is always on stage—is part of the image you convey to your audience."[2]

Communication is occurring so long as people attach meanings to what's going on around them. Anything we do (or fail to do) can potentially communicate *something* to others.

INTRODUCTION: GRABS YOU, ALIGNS YOU, LOCKS YOU IN

The advertisement for a television set that "takes the color, grabs it, aligns it, and locks it in" pretty well describes what a good introduction should do. The introduction that just gets attention does only part of the job. You can get attention by pounding on the desk, tapping a waterglass with a spoon, shouting obscenities, or telling an ethnic joke, but that doesn't serve as an introduction *unless* it also leads the audience into the body of the talk.

The introduction is not just an addendum we tack on the beginning of a talk. It serves several important purposes. These purposes include—

1. getting the audience's attention
2. preparing the audience for the theme of the presentation (creating expectations)
3. establishing credibility

In addition to these, an introduction *may* also

1. disclose the central theme
2. limit the scope of the presentation
3. directly state a conclusion

Whether or not you will do all these things in your introduction will depend upon your purpose, topic, and relationship to the audience. We'll talk about techniques for getting attention in a moment, and we've discussed credibility in Chapter 5. But let's consider the idea of creating listener expectations for a moment.

Each of us goes into communication situations with a certain mental set—some expectations of what it will be like. A colleague of mine[3] uses the following game in the classroom to illustrate how we can *create* expectations in others. You may want to try this on someone.

The instructor asks a question and requests the whole class to spell the answers three times out loud. He then quickly asks a follow-up question.

Instructor: There was a U.S. President whose name rhymes with "folk." Who was he?
Students: Polk
Instructor: Ok, let's spell it 3 times. P-O-L-K; P-O-L-K; P-O-L-K. What do you call the white of an egg?
Students: Yolk

Instructor: There were certain structures that the pioneers built to protect themselves from indian attacks. What do you call such a structure?
Students: Fort
Instructor: Ok, let's spell it 3 times. F-O-R-T; F-O-R-T; F-O-R-T. What do you eat your soup with?
Students: A fork.

Instructor: A forest is made up of a whole bunch of what?
Students: Trees.
Instructor: Ok, let's spell tree 3 times. T-R-E-E; T-R-E-E; T-R-E-E. How many of each animal did Moses take into the ark with him? (By now the students feel they've caught on to the game. About half the group will say "three" while others will say "two.") The correct answer is that *Moses* didn't have an ark, it was *Noah*.

The exercise (which, by the way, has worked perfectly every time I've tried it) points out how mental set can be established and how it can affect listener responses. People will hear what they expect to hear unless a speaker is very careful to create awareness that something different is going to be said.

Here is an example of a speaker's opening remarks which create appropriate expectations by telling exactly what will be covered. This is also an example of a *direct* order of arrangement as discussed in Chapter 6. The topic of the presentation was tax reform.

> In this particular talk I shall suggest a specific program to restore a favorable investment climate. Some aspects of this program are a challenge, so I ask you to consider it all as a package. This program involves, among other things, a higher personal income tax, a lower capital gains tax, a new approach to investment credit based upon taxes before application of investment credit, continuation of tax-free bonds, a return of interest from a fully deductible expense and a continuing use of special tax preferences. Now the logic to support this program.[4]

"*Chief, I have good news and bad news. The bad news couldn't be worse and the good news couldn't be better. I also have some in-between news that couldn't be more so-so.*"

Providing your listeners with appropriate expectations will help them to understand your message.

TECHNIQUES FOR INTRODUCING YOUR TALK

Let's look now at some proven ways to gain audience attention and create appropriate expectations. The purpose of your talk, nature of your audience, and your personality should all be considered when developing the introduction. The vast majority of business presentations I've witnessed fail to use the potential power of a first-rate introduction. Let's consider some of the options available.

1. *Statement of purpose:* There are times when a simple statement of what you'll be covering is an adequate opening remark—but not many! Too often we hear lukewarm statements like "Jack asked me to say a few words about . . ." or "I'm going to cover the policy change dealing with . . ."

    Just writing these makes me want to yawn! Of all the readily available introductory techniques, this is the weakest—and the most frequently used. Its main drawback is that unless the topic is of some *vital* interest to your listeners (and they recognize it as such) you simply won't bind your listeners to you. You are offering them little or no incentive to listen by simply stating what you are going to do. Try another approach and you'll be miles ahead.

2. *Provocative or startling statement:* Instead of saying "I'm going to explain the new sales compensation program," why not spark their imaginations with a

106

statement like this: "In the next 15 minutes I'm going to explain how each one of you can increase your earnings by 50 percent this year." I guarantee, you'll get their attention with that.

I can still remember a startling statement made by a classmate of mine 15 years ago to open a talk on water pollution. He said, in a very matter of fact tone, "The Buffalo River has been declared a fire hazard."

"How the heck can a *river* be a *fire hazard?*" I asked myself. And he had my attention!

These kinds of straightforward statements can get your listeners' attention if they are interestingly worded and not too complicated. Avoid the temptation to be overly dramatic. A good provocative statement stands alone without a tone of voice that implies a big exclamation point.

Your listeners' reactions to such a statement is to perk up and mentally ask for more information. Now your audience is participating with you and you're on the way to establishing understanding.

3. *Statistics:* Closely related to the provocative statement—in fact it can be one form of such a statement—is the presentation of a statistic. "Today more than 64 percent of our female employees utilize day care facilities for their children at a cost of more than $90,000 per year." Or, this one I recently heard:

> The Tax Foundation reports that the average American works an hour and 27 minutes each day to pay for housing and household operations. Food and beverages take another hour and three minutes. Clothing takes 23 minutes, transportation costs 42 minutes and medical care an average of 30 minutes. But that's only peanuts. The biggest bite of all is taken by federal, state, and local government. Combined they absorb a staggering 34.4 percent of earnings of all Americans—or roughly, two hours and 45 minutes of each work day to pay various taxes.

These kinds of statistics can be real "grabbers."

Be careful in your use of statistics. They can be rather slippery when used carelessly or unethically. Almost anyone can take statistical data and present them in different ways to imply quite different conclusions. I recall that during the 1976 presidential campaign, Jimmy Carter was stressing *unemployment* statistics while President Ford was using the same data to show that a record number of Americans *had jobs.*

Nevertheless, people find statistics interesting, and will pay attention to clearly expressed statistical information that is relevant to them.

4. *Rhetorical question:* A rhetorical question is a thought-provoking question for which you don't expect to get an answer. "Just how much more government interference can our company take?" or "How would you feel if you were turned down for a promotion because your skin was not the right color?" Sometimes a whole series of these is effective. "What will you do (a) when there

is no gasoline to drive your car? (b) when there is no fuel to heat your home? (c) when our electrical generators go silent? (d) when the oil supply runs out?"

"What will you do?"

Be careful not to overwork this approach. And remember that there is always the danger that some wise guy will *answer* your questions and completely deflate your introduction: "How many more people do we have to lose to competition before we wake up?" If someone in the audience deadpans, "eleven," your intro may fizzle.

5.   *Quotation, definition or short narrative:* Often a short story, quote or light remark can effectively lead into the body of your talk. A briefing advocating expenditures for additional training might build upon a quote from Benjamin Franklin who said, "If a man empties his purse into his head no man can take it away from him." If a man invests in learning he has made the greatest investment." Other examples of quotes and definitions are found at the beginning of each chapter of this book.

Here's an example I recently heard. A newspaper editor was critical of President Jimmy Carter's call for personal sacrifice to solve the inflation. He began this way:

> Chutzpah is a Yiddish word for nerve or gall. It's best defined by the story of the boy who murders his parents and then begs for the mercy of the court on the grounds that he's an orphan.
>
> You've got chutzpah, Mr. President.
>
> Our government wrecks our pocketbooks and ruins our dollar. Then our president goes on TV and appeals to us to put the house in order.
>
> Some nerve, some gall.

Everybody loves to hear a story. So it is no surprise that the narrative or short anecdote, especially if it is a personal example, often works beautifully. Simply relate your interesting experiences as though you were telling a friend. Strive for a conversational tone. Don't drag out the story. Use it only as a lead-in to the meat of your talk.

Some people are hesitant about using personal examples. They shouldn't be. Firsthand experiences have vitality and can be explained more clearly than secondhand stories. George Bernard Shaw wasn't shy about using personal examples. He once said, "I often quote myself. It adds spice to my conversations."

You need not be a professional entertainer to come up with useful attention-getting materials. Your local library will have dozens of books of humor and interesting anecdotes which are likely to fit into your theme. I'll discuss ways to liven up a talk with humor and entertaining asides in Chapter 8.

6.   *Audience participation:* Last, but definitely not least, you may want to use audience participation in your introduction. Asking a few key questions of

specific audience members or having the group take a quiz or participate in a simple game may be the best way to get them in tune with your presentation.

"I'd like to ask for your candid remarks about the new building proposals. Martha, what concerns do you have?" Be sure you don't put people on the spot. Be sensitive to your tone of voice in asking the questions. Don't do anything that's likely to embarrass your listeners or make them uncomfortable. In short, use this approach with discretion. Don't drag it out too long, and be sure to show your listeners how this relates to your theme and purpose.

The keyword in developing effective introductions is *creativity*. Resist the path of least resistance—the simple statement of your purpose—if there are any more interesting ways open to you. And there usually are some available.

SURE-FIRE WAYS TO FLOP

An inadequate introduction can seriously damage your talk by failing to gain attention, setting an inappropriate theme and destroying your credibility. Here are some sure-fire ways to fall on your face.

1. *The apologetic beginning:* Start out by saying something like "unaccustomed as I am to public speaking, I . . ." or "I'm here to bore you with a few

"Will the meeting please come to order and will you pick a card, J.B., any card, look at it and return it face down to the deck . . ."

ROTHCO

Getting your listeners to participate can be a good attention-getter. But be sure it's relevant to your talk.

Source: © 1978 Punch/Rothco.

more statistics," or "I'm pretty nervous, so I hope you'll bear with me." If you haven't prepared well enough to be effective, it will become obvious to your audience soon enough. You accomplish nothing by announcing it.

2. *The potentially offensive beginning:* An off-color joke or ridiculing statement will eventually get you in trouble. You never know for sure how someone will respond to an off-color, sarcastic or otherwise potentially offensive remark. Avoid them. You have nothing to gain from their use and much to lose.

3. *The same opening regardless of audience or occasion:* Also, be careful of getting into the habit of using the same opening for all occasions. The story is told of a rather timid governor who spoke to the inmates of a men's penitentiary. He began conventionally with "Ladies and . . ." but there was laughter before he could get out the word "gentlemen." After he recovered, he began a second time with "Fellow inmates," and again there was a burst of laughter. A moment later he blundered on with "Glad to see so many of you here."

Other openings may be inappropriate because they are trite or excessively flattering, or just plain phoney: "I am filled with a deep sense of personal inadequacy when I presume to speak authoritatively in the presence of so many knowledgable men." Ugh!

4. *The gimmicky beginning:* Some people carry creativity a bit too far and come up with gimmicks that fizzle. People who blow whistles, act out scenes from a play, honk horns or write the word SEX on the blackboard saying "now that I have your attention . . ." run a serious risk of damaging their credibility. These kinds of things tend to put your audience on the spot—they don't know how to respond. It's embarrassing and distracting. Avoid any gimmick that may confuse your listeners or make them feel uncomfortable. They may not forgive you for it.

5. *The artificial or pointless beginning:* Some speakers try too hard to be cute and, as with the gimmicky beginning, confuse the audience and hurt the speaker's credibility. The following example appears in a book by Phillips and Zolten.

> Dear Friends, it is so good to be with you here today speaking to you, and I hope you will find my remarks interesting. That reminds me of the story of the two men who were walking down the street and one said to the other, "Why does a chicken cross the road?" and the other replied, "That was no chicken, that was my wife." Well, ladies and gentlemen, I'm no chicken, but I hope that my speech will make you my wife in a manner of speaking, because maybe we can have a wedding about the topic I am speaking on today. We need to get married on the idea that the prime interest rate needs to come down.[5]

A good introduction can be a powerful tool. Keep in mind your purposes (gain attention, create expectations, and build credibility) and apply your creativity. It'll be well worth the effort.

TRANSITIONS: HERE'S HOW THIS FITS TOGETHER

Transition words or phrases provide the links that hold the talk together. Typically they do one or more of the following:

- briefly recap or summarize what's just been covered;
- suggest, imply, or state what is to come next;
- lead into a conclusion.

Ted Frank and David Ray,[6] in their recent book, suggest that transitional phrases help us avoid an "I'm sorry, you just lost me" response from our listeners. They cite four categories of transitional phrases and give examples of each. Note that each word or phrase is followed by a series of periods (ellipses) indicating that something is to be added. When you say, "of even greater appeal . . ." followed by a short pause, the brief silence permits your listener to trigger an appropriate expectation about what will be said next.

Inference. When you want to demonstrate that you have drawn a conclusion from your examples, transitional words or phrases that help link this inference include:

For this reason . .	On that account . . .	As a result . . .
To this end . . .	The consequence is . . .	It follows that. . .
In this way . . .	By looking at it this way . . .	Naturally . . .
Thus . . .	Accordingly . . .	In order that . . .

Change of Time. Because most people have had lots of experience dealing with narratives that chronicle events, the transitional phrases that show time are probably familiar to you. How many of these transitions do you routinely use in telling an account of an experience?

Now . . .	Meanwhile . . .	At present . . .
Immediately . . .	At last . . .	Since then . . .
After a short time . . .	Afterwards . . .	Not long after . . .
Instantly . . .	Quickly . . .	In the meantime . . .
Before this . . .	Shortly after . . .	At this point . . .
Later . . .	Whereupon . . .	Suddenly . . .

Comparison and Personal View. Many times you will search for a way to compare an idea to something else, but you may also wish to show your own posture in the comparison or your manner of approaching the differences and/or similarities. Some of these phrases might help:

Equally important . . .	More effective . . .	Quite as necessary . . .
Not so obvious . . .	In like manner . . .	Of even greater appeal . . .
Just as surely . . .	Likewise . . .	In similar fashion . . .

As you would expect . . .   Quite as evident . . .   Accordingly . . .

On the other hand . . .   Conversely . . .   In contrast . . .

Doubt or Certainty. Transitions that lead into a state of doubt or of certainty might be introduced with one of these words:

Possibly . . .	Perhaps . . .	It may well be . . .
Probably . . .	Obviously . . .	Undoubtedly . . .
Surely . . .	Of course . . .	However . . .
Still . . .	Yet . . .	Nevertheless . . .
Furthermore . . .		

Transitional words and phrases help your listeners shift gears, readjust expectations and mentally recap what has been covered. Without adequate transitions it is almost impossible for listeners to follow even a moderately complex line of thought. But you as the speaker also get important advantages from the liberal use of transitions. They give you extra moments to check your notes, change physical position, re-establish eye contact with your audience, check for listener feedback, or adjust a visual aid.

SUMMARIES AND CONCLUSIONS: HERE'S WHAT YOU NEED TO REMEMBER

Four things should be accomplished as you end most presentations. (The exception may be the simple progress report.) You should

1. summarize key points
2. restate your central theme
3. point to the listeners' need to know what you've just told them and remind them of the urgency (or at least importance) of that information, and
4. provide them with a clear action step, a prescribed behavior or mental activity they should *do.*

Summaries are especially useful here to recap the *key ideas* (but not too many details) of your talk. Keep in mind how repetition helps us remember; then use this important tool one more time as you lead into your close. Avoid introducing any new material at this point. It may confuse your listeners.

Everything you have done to develop this presentation comes to a climax at the conclusion. So a most important question goes back to your conceptual planning—what was your specific intent? Picture yourself as a listener and ask the tough question: "What does this all mean to me?" Your talk should have provided a clear answer. *Action steps* are appropriate for all kinds of briefings. Your audience has a right to expect and receive guidance from all your research and preparation. And if you don't provide such guidance in the form of a clear, action-oriented conclusion, you have probably let your listeners down. The actions you advocate should, of course, be ones you can realistically request from your listeners.

Your conclusions need not be elaborate or drawn out. If the rest of the talk is well done, the conclusion will be self-evident and you need only restate and bring a sense of finality.

An effective presentation begins with a creative introduction that gains attention and binds your listeners to you. The liberal use of transitions ties together what you are saying and leads up to a strong conclusion. These are crucial to getting your thoughts across.

BEGINNINGS, TRANSITIONS AND ENDINGS: THE TIES THAT BIND

Chapter 7. A summary of key ideas

1. Communication is not something we can totally turn on or off. Anything we do can provide potential cues to others which they attach meanings to. We communicate (usually nonverbally) even before we get up to give a talk.
2. The introduction serves to
   (a) gain listener attention
   (b) prepare the audience for the theme of the talk by creating expectations
   (c) establish credibility for the speaker.
3. Some introductions may also
   (a) disclose the central theme of the talk
   (b) define or limit the scope of the talk
   (c) directly state a conclusion.
4. Speakers can create mental set or expectations in their audience. Doing so can enhance the probability of accurate communication.
5. Six techniques for introducing a talk include
   (a) statement of purpose
   (b) provocative or startling statement
   (c) statistics
   (d) rhetorical question
   (e) quotation, definition, or short narrative
   (f) audience participation.

6. There are at least five "sure-fire ways to flop" with your introduction. These include

    (a) the apologetic beginning
    (b) the potentially offensive beginning
    (c) the same opening regardless of audience or occasion
    (d) the gimmicky beginning
    (e) the artificial or pointless beginning.

7. Transition words and phrases link the talk together and help both the listener and the speaker organize their thoughts.

8. Summaries tie together key points and lead into the conclusion. Four things should be accomplished as you end a presentation. You should

    (a) summarize key points
    (b) restate your central theme
    (c) remind the listeners of their need to know
    (d) provide a clear action step.

9. Action steps are appropriate for all kinds of briefings; your audience has a right to expect and receive guidance from you.

NOTES

1. Paul Preston. *Communication for Managers* (Englewood Cliffs, NJ: Prentice-Hall, 1979), p. 91.
2. Ibid., p. 92.
3. Dr. Al W. Switzler, a professor in the Graduate School of Management at Brigham Young University taught me this exercise.
4. From a speech by Ira G. Corn, Jr., Chief Executive Officer of Michigan General addressing the National Institute in Dallas. Reprinted in *Vital Speeches of the Day*, July 15, 1974, p. 584.
5. Gerald M. Phillips and J. Jerome Zolten. *Structuring Speech* (Indianapolis: Bobbs-Merrill, 1976), p. 233.
6. Ted Frank, David Ray, *Basic Business and Professional SPEECH Communication,* © 1979, p. 177–178. Reprinted by permission of Prentice-Hall, Inc.

8

ADD A LITTLE LIFE TO YOUR STYLE:
holding listener interest

OBJECTIVES OF CHAPTER 8

After studying this chapter, the reader should be able to:

1. Describe the function of affective language and explain how it differs from reporting language.
2. Explain and give examples of "direct address" or "this means you" statements.
3. Describe and give examples of the use of metaphor, simile, and hyperbole as affective devices.
4. Name and give examples of eight humorous devices.
5. Explain and give an example of how explicit, unembellished facts can arouse powerful emotional reactions in listeners.

Most people have sat through talks that were well organized, carefully prepared, skillfully delivered but, in a word, *boring*. "It wasn't my fault. It was just a dull topic." is the speaker's most common defense. But I'm not sure that argument holds water. Almost any topic can be made interesting to your listeners. In this chapter I'll discuss some techniques for gaining and holding listener interest.

AFFECTIVE LANGUAGE CONVEYS FEELINGS

One way such interest is often developed is through what S.I. Hayakawa calls "the language of *affective communication.*" This type of word usage goes beyond purely factual information. Hayakawa contrasts it with report language.

> The language of reports is instrumental in getting done the work necessary for life, but it does not tell us anything about what life feels like in the living. We can communicate scientific facts to each other without knowing or caring about each other's feelings; but before love, friendship, and community can be established among men so that we will *want* to cooperate and become a society, there must be, as we have seen, a flow of sympathy between one man and another. This flow of sympathy is established, of course, by means of the affective uses of language. Most of the time, after all, we are not interested in keeping our feelings out of our discourse, but rather we are eager to express them as fully as we can.[1]

Hayakawa then goes on to talk about several ways to express feelings through affective language. Although some of the things he suggests are more frequently applied to literature or poetry, many of the ideas are useful to the business speaker who wants to "add life" to a talk. Expressions of feeling convey urgency or enthusiasm which is likely to be contagious—your audience will "catch the vision" of what you say when they better understand your feelings.

DIRECT ADDRESS OR "THIS MEANS YOU" STATEMENTS

One affective device is simply direct address, to the listener. The speaker makes "this means you!" type statements. Each day we see examples of this approach in television and radio commercials. The announcer "personally" addresses each of the several million people who may be listening and attempts to make them feel that he or she is speaking to them as individuals. The direct address technique is now also common in the written media. Computers have been taught to program letters to include the name of the addressee several places within the body of the message. The "personal letters" have been shown to be very effective in helping to raise funds for political candidates, and getting people to enter the *Reader's Digest* sweepstakes.

Direct address shows your listeners how your message applies to them and how it can meet their individual needs in some way. This technique relates closely to the notion of tying "features" to "benefits" used by sales representatives. A feature is a characteristic of the product being sold (this copy machine can duplicate on both sides of a sheet of paper). The benefit is a "what this means to you, Mr. Customer" statement (you can cut your postage and paper costs by up to 50 percent). I'll talk more about features and benefits in Chapter 11. For now, remember that personalizing your message by telling the listener that this applies to his or her specific interests and needs is an important and simple technique for holding interest.

FIGURATIVE LANGUAGE

Another affective element is the use of figurative language devices such as metaphor, simile, and hyperbole. Figurative expressions are frequently useful because they conjure up a humorous or thought-provoking image in the mind of the listener. Although they may be nonsensical if interpreted literally, they nevertheless can make a great deal of sense when we hear them spoken figuratively. *Hyperbole* is the use of an intentional exaggeration not expected to be taken literally. Expressions such as "the purchasing agent has *a basket full of money* to spend on office equipment," or "Harry wouldn't recognize a bargain if *it carried a neon sign,*" or "by the time he finished speaking the audience was *comatose*" make a point in an imprecise but rather interesting way. Be careful to avoid cliches which deaden the effect. Look for fresh, imaginative expressions.

Metaphor is used to figuratively suggest a resemblance between things that are not literally associated. Educator John Dewey is credited with this metaphor that effectively conveyed his feelings about the process of IQ testing:

> This intelligence-testing business reminds me of the way they used to weigh hogs in Texas. They would get a long plank, put it over a cross-bar, and somehow tie the hog on one end of the plank. They'd search all around till they found a stone that would balance the weight of the hog and they'd put that on the other end of the plank. Then, they'd guess the weight of the stone.

A metaphor like that one has power! It not only makes a talk more interesting but it'll stick with the listeners long after your talk is over.

Simile is a figurative comparison usually using the terms "like" or "as." In simile, we would avoid saying "he is a moose," (hyperbole) and instead say "He is *like* a moose."

Many figurative expressions are used so frequently that they become trite or overworked to the extent of being nearly meaningless. Expressions such as "a horse of a different color," "mind-boggling," "head shrinker," "dead-wood," "bottom line," and many other terms fall in this category.

Another danger in the use of metaphor, simile, and hyperbole lies in the fact that they express direct evaluations; they are likely to reveal strong feelings in a less than objective way. Doing so, you run the risk of a backlash from a listener who doesn't agree with your overstated conclusion. Since metaphoric expressions often reflect oversimplification, says Hayakawa, "they are to be found in special abundance, therefore, in all primitive speech, in folk speech, in speech of the unlearned, in the speech of children, and in the professional argot of theater people, of gangsters, and of those in other lively occupations."[2]

So what does all this mean for the business speaker? Metaphor, hyperbole, and simile can add life to your style but they do so at the cost of technical accuracy and objectivity. A clever and original metaphor can be fun to use and helpful to your audience. An overworked one will have no benefit and may even irritate your listeners. As Fred Allen said,

> Hush, little bright line, don't you cry.
> You'll be a cliche by and by.

Humorist Percy H. Whiting wrote a book based on his many years of experience called *How to Speak and Write with Humor*. His advice includes these comments:

> The surest way *never* to achieve brightness or wit in writing, conversation, or public speaking is to depend for your laughs on cliches and slang—on the worn-out humor of somebody else.
>
> People use cliches, slang, and profanity because they are too lazy to think up equivalent expressions of their own. So they use phrases that others invented and thus lose the chance to get practice in making humorous remarks. This "lazy man's language" can be produced by a man with a reasonably good memory, substantially without mental effort.[3]

At another place in his book, Whiting says, "as long as you are satisfied to dish up your humor warmed over—you will never get any practice at being funny, and practice is what you need . . . . If you refrain from slang and other

"To illustrate my point, gentlemen, I'm going to tell a little joke, and I want you to laugh at it as if you'd never heard it before and your job depended upon it."

Humor is one excellent way to hold listener interest. . . .

forms of cliche, you will force yourself to use your own mind instead of your memory."[4] Let's talk about some principles of humor which each of us can creatively adapt to speaking situations.

DON'T TELL JOKES—USE WIT

The most interesting and entertaining people I know never tell jokes, at least not in the "Did ya hear the one about . . ." sense of that term. They do, however, spice up their conversation with humorous devices.

Although it goes beyond the scope of this book to analyze theories of humor, I'd like to name several techniques and give one or two examples of each to provoke your thoughts about what kinds of things tend to be funny to your listeners. But first a few words on being funny—and interesting.

Most business presentations—or any kind of communication for that matter—can be improved by a little wit. But being funny does not come naturally to anyone. It has to be learned and it's hard work. Yet anyone can learn to say funny things in large part by applying certain humorous devices in original and creative ways.

The next time you hear a humorous remark or story or you read cartoons like the ones in this book, *analyze* them and try to figure out what makes them funny. More often than not, you'll find one of the following techniques at work:

The incongruous list. This is one of the easier techniques to use. It involves simply including a totally incongruous item in a list of serious items. If the item is sufficiently ridiculous, you'll get a good laugh. One recent cartoon showed a dignified gentleman addressing what appeared to be a corporate board of directors saying,

"Gentlemen, my talk today is entitled 'Corporate Responsibility, Sound Fiscal Policy, and Farrah Fawcett-Majors.' "

This technique is easy to use. Simply look through your talk and see where you've used a list of articles or events—then slip in one ridiculous item. Often a shift in language formality makes this technique work as in another cartoon I recently saw. An employee was saying to his boss,

"I don't want a raise, Mr. Williford. I just want bouquets and accolades and tokens of esteem and bravos and huzzahs and a piece of the action."

Here is one more example from a cartoon.

Man listening to a taped message on the telephone: "The time is 3:10 pm. The temperature is 72. The air quality is acceptable. The barometer is 29.94. The fish are jumpin' and the cotton is high."

Exaggeration. This can also add vitality to your speech *provided the audience knows you are kidding.* You have to make the exaggerated part so absurd that no one would mistakenly think you're serious. This technique has long been a mainstay of American humor from the "tall tales" of Paul Bunyon and Big John Henry to the writings of modern-day humorists. Like the incongruous list item, exaggeration can be thrown into a talk almost anywhere without having to "set up" your listeners that a joke is coming. The element of surprise makes it fun to use.

A radio announcer caught me off guard when he informed listeners, the day after a particularly violent thunder shower, that "there's a 40 percent chance of afternoon and evening thunder showers with winds gusting from 15 to 3,000 miles per hour!"

A business executive estimated that our total annual profits will drop to "about eleven cents" if sales don't pick up. In my salesman days I heard of one executive's secretary who was so mean she'd "wrestle you to the ground" before letting you see the boss without an appointment.

Practice exaggeration. "Don't just *mildly* exaggerate—make it preposterous. Any speech that will be improved by a bit of humor is a good place to use exaggeration . . . [but] *don't overdo it.* Too much exaggeration is tiresome."[5]

Juxtaposition. Adding an inappropriate, out-of-place, or inconsistent item or comment can provoke humor if it throws one off the train of thought and creates surprise. This technique works essentially the same as the incongruous list. Notice how humorist Woody Allen juxtaposes a religious theme with the temporal.

"If only God would give me some clear sign! Like making a large deposit in my name at a Swiss bank."

"I don't want to achieve immortality through my work. I want to achieve it through not dying."

Here's another variation of juxtaposition.

"How you getting along?" the veteran salesperson asked the fledgling.

"Rotten. I got nothing but insults every place I called."

"That's funny," the old man mused. "I been on the road 40 years. I've had doors slammed in my face, my samples dumped in the street. I been tossed down stairs, been manhandled by janitors—but insulted? Never!"[6]

Humorous quote or definition. Any library will have several books of quotations, many of them witty, which can spice up a presentation. Often these use the techniques of juxtaposition, exaggeration, or incongruous lists already mentioned. One of the more recent sources of these was compiled by Lawrence J. Peter: *Peter's Quotations: Ideas For Our Time.*[7] It's available in paperback and can be a very useful reference.

I've used quotes or definitions throughout this book in an attempt to gain and sustain interest for my readers. Here are a few more:

"The business of government is to keep the government out of business—that is, unless business needs government aid."

Will Rogers

George Gobel's definition of a salesman: "A fellow with a smile on his face, a shine on his shoes, and a lousy territory."

An efficiency expert is a guy who is smart enough to tell you how to run your business and too smart to start his own.

I've found interesting quotable quotes in a wide range of sources from *Sports Illustrated* to *The Bible.* Almost every book will have a few. It's a good idea to keep a pack of $3 \times 5''$ cards handy to jot these down when you come across them. Then toss the cards into a file box and use them as the occasion arises.

Insult. This is one of the oldest forms of humor and one that is still popular. Comedians like Don Rickles make their living insulting others. But insults should be used carefully lest we cross the line between making fun and hurting someone's feelings. Most listeners can take a good-natured barb that deflates the ego a bit. I recently heard a speaker talking about his boss who sat at the head table next to him as he spoke.

"Folks, I want you to know that my boss, Pete Zaleski, is a fine leader, a sensitive and effective supervisor, a friend, a counselor, a skillful executive, an honest man, a man of great intelligence . . ." (pause) The speaker then turned to his boss holding his speech notes and said, "Pete, what else does this say. I can't read your writing."

A friend of mine cheerfully insulted the membership of the Rotary Club to whom he was speaking by announcing that he had always had the greatest respect for Rotary—"In fact, I even bought one of your lawn mowers!"

Comedian Henny Youngman is a master of the putdown.

"Some people bring happiness wherever they go. You bring happiness whenever you go."

"Where were you when I needed you? I looked high and low. I guess I didn't look low enough."

The popular TV "roasts" have taken the insult to new heights (or depths). I heard of a roast of a professor by some students that concluded (after citing all the educator's eccentricities) by excusing him his many shortcomings since it was widely known that Professor X "was insane." That barb may have crossed the line between good natured insult and slander. (Then again, it may have hit too close to home!) Be very careful if you use the insult as a humorous technique. Raymond Ross reminds us that the insult or satirical humor "is a two-edged sword that may cut deeper than intended, miss the mark, or decapitate the source on the return swing!"[8]

The anticlimax. When you use a "sudden collapse from a serious crescendo and that falloff in dignity is so extreme as to be ludicrous"[9] you are using anticlimax. Often the tone and language provide an ideal setup for the anticlimactic shift. Here are some examples:

A demure young bride, a trifle pale, her lips set in a tremulous smile, slowly stepped down the long church aisle on the arm of her dignified but aging father.
As she reached the low platform before the altar, her tiny slippered foot brushed a potted fern, upsetting it. She looked down at the spilled dirt seriously, and her childlike eyes rose to the sedate fact of the minister.
"That," she said, "is a hell of a place to put a plant!"[10]

Often, the quotes of others use the device. Here's one by Mark Twain.

"In our country, we have three unspeakably precious things: freedom of speech, freedom of conscience and the prudence not to practice either."

Understatement. Closely related to the anticlimax is understatement. Again, there is a "sudden collapse from a crescendo" when you lead up to a potentially powerful point and then present that point in restrained terms. Your conclusion is represented less strongly than the facts would bear out.
George Santayana's quote about philosophy is a classic.
"It is a great advantage for a system of philosophy to be substantially true."

Another example was seen on a recent television awards program. Songwriter Don Schlitz (who wrote the Kenny Rogers' hit *The Gambler)* used this technique beautifully. Schlitz had just won the Country Music Association's award for *best song of the year!* As he came forth to accept the prestigious award he said, "You know, this is the first song I've ever had recorded." (Pause; then in a matter-of-fact tone:) "I find this encouraging."

When the facts and reasoning presented are exceptionally strong, an understated conclusion can be powerful, as well as interesting.

The play on words. One final humor and interest technique is the play on words. Occasionally these work. But often, in oral communication, they miss the mark. The pun (one form of play on words) can be dangerous. Either they bypass the listeners entirely or, when recognized, elicit a groan. I personally enjoy puns, but they are very difficult to use in oral presentations. Nevertheless, here are examples of word plays I heard years ago which have stuck with me:

During the 1968 Presidential election campaign, comedian Pat Paulson proclaimed, "I'm not a right winger nor a left winger. I'm sort of middle of the bird."

Horse sense is stable thinking.

The Henny Youngman line: "You're a contact man, all right. All con and no tact."

Many humorous devices overlap the categories I've described and incorporate several gimmicks. The best advice for putting lively humor into a presentation is to plan it, prepare it and practice it. Avoid the use of cliches or worn out phrases. Then experiment with ways of humorizing your talks to give them sparkle and interest.

THE AFFECTIVENESS OF FACTS

Having discussed direct address, metaphor and humor let me remind you that these are not the only ways to gain and hold listener interest. Although each of these techniques for arousing listener involvement are useful in their place, often the most powerful emotional reactions can come from objectively presented facts themselves. When factual data is presented very explicitly and very clearly it can lead the listener to the conclusion you are trying to make without additional affective techniques. Here is an example. The following account of an automobile accident is quoted from the *Chicago Sun-Times:*

One [victim], Alex Kuzma, 63, of 808 North Maplewood Avenue, was hit with such impact that his right forearm was carried off on the car of the hit-run motorist who struck him. Kuzma was struck Sunday as he crossed Chicago Avenue at Campbell Avenue. Witnesses saw the car slow down, douse its headlights and speed away. After searching futilely for the dead man's missing arm, police expressed belief it must have lodged in some section of the speeding auto.

There are few readers who will not have some kind of affective reaction to this story—at least a mild horror at the gruesomeness of the accident and some indignation at the driver who failed to stop after striking someone. Facts themselves, especially at lower levels of abstraction, can be affective without the use of special literary devices to make them more so.[11]

One further example—a classic example—of the power of stating externally observable facts in the form of bare reports and of letting the reported facts have their impact on the reader. The following is the famous ending of Ernest Hemingway's *A Farewell to Arms:*

I went into the room and stayed with Catherine until she died. She was unconscious all the time, and it did not take her very long to die.

Outside the room, in the hall, I spoke to the doctor, "Is there anything I can do tonight?"

"No. There is nothing to do. Can I take you to your hotel?"
"No, thank you. I am going to stay here a while."
"I know there is nothing to say. I cannot tell you—"
"No," I said. "There's nothing to say."
"Goodnight," he said. "I cannot take you to your hotel?"
"No, thank you."
"It was the only thing to do," he said. "The operation proved—"
"I do not want to talk about it," I said.
"I would like to take you to your hotel."
"No, thank you."
He went down the hall. I went to the door of the room.
"You can't come in now," one of the nurses said.
"Yes I can," I said.
"You can't come in yet."
"You get out," I said. "The other one too."
But after I had got them out and shut the door and turned off the light it wasn't any good. It was like saying good-by to a statue. After a while I went out and left the hospital and walked back to the hotel in the rain.

The creative use of a variety of interest-building devices is a key to effective speaking. Some of the best speakers I know can shift smoothly from wit to the affectiveness of facts. Holding your listeners' interest is an art, not a science. In this chapter we've suggested some devices that, when skillfully used, can "add a little life to your style." Try them. See how your listeners react.

ADD A LITTLE LIFE TO YOUR STYLE:
HOLDING LISTENER INTEREST

Chapter 8. A summary of key ideas

1. Affective language conveys more than factual data; it expresses feelings.
2. Direct address or the use of "this means you" statements personalizes messages for listeners.
3. Metaphor, hyperbole, and simile conjure up thought-provoking images which hold listener interest.
4. Some figurative expressions are overused and become trite. Avoid use of cliches and other overused phrases. Achieve brightness or wit in expression by being original.
5. Wit can be developed through creative use of light humorous devices.
    (a) the incongruous list
    (b) exaggeration
    (c) juxtaposition
    (d) humorous quote or definition
    (e) the insult
    (f) anticlimax
    (g) understatement
    (h) the play on words
6. Powerful emotional reactions can arise from explicitly presented and unembellished facts.
7. Creative use of a variety of interest-building devices is a key to speaking effectiveness.

NOTES

1. S.I. Hayakawa. *Language in Thought and Action,* 3rd ed. (New York: Harcourt Brace Jovanovich, Inc., 1972), pp. 102–3.
2. Ibid., p. 106

3. Percy H. Whiting. *How to Speak and Write With Humor* (New York: McGraw-Hill, 1959), p. 117.
4. Ibid., p. 23.
5. Ibid., p. 43.
6. *The Reader's Digest Treasury of American Humor* (Reader's Digest Association, 1972), p. 131.
7. Lawrence J. Peter. *Peter's Quotations: Ideas For Our Time* (New York: Morrow, 1977).
8. Raymond Ross. *Persuasion: Communication and Interpersonal Relations* (Englewood Cliffs, NJ: Prentice-Hall, Inc., 1974), p. 163.
9. Whiting, p. 67.
10. Whiting, p. 70.
11. Hayakawa, p. 111.

9

VISUAL AIDS:
sharpen key points, focus the picture

OBJECTIVES OF CHAPTER 9

After studying this chapter, the reader should be able to:

1. Name four ways visual aids help the speaker.
2. Describe how the planning and use of visuals can help the speaker in conceptual planning, development of content, and delivery of the presentation.
3. Identify six types of direct visuals and give examples of their use.
4. Name seven key rules for the effective use of direct visuals.
5. Name the two most common types of projected visuals and describe their advantages over direct visuals.
6. Name five suggestions for the effective use of projected visuals.

Most people are poor visualizers. The majority of the people we communicate with today were raised in the TV generation. We're not accustomed to processing spoken information alone—we need to *see* something too. There is a significant difference between just telling and showing while telling.

Numerous studies of listener comprehension repeatedly come to the same conclusion: visual aids help listeners get the message. Typical of these studies was one by Robert S. Craig of the U.S. Public Health Service who reported at a national health conference that "when knowledge was imparted to a person by *telling alone,* the recall three hours later was 70 percent, and three days later only 10 percent." When *showing alone* was used, "the knowledge recall three hours later was 72 percent, and three days later about 35 percent." However, when *both telling and showing* were the teaching tools, the recall three hours later was 85 percent, and three days later 65 percent.[1]

Robert L. Montgomery, a veteran teacher of public speaking, strongly encourages heavy use of visual aids. He relates that "the American Management Association, which has been training people in management throughout the world since 1923, says that they have found through testing that there is only a 10 percent return on an average lecture, but this percentage jumps to as high as 50 percent when a presentation has been made with visual aids. And this percentage hits 70 percent when there are visual aids and audience participation as well."[2]

The use of audio-visual materials came into prominence during World War II when the military services were faced with a tremendous task of quickly and efficiently training millions of people. Men and women of different educational backgrounds had to be trained in many different skills needed for the war effort. And this training had to be done quickly and thoroughly. Social scientists then found that about 85 percent of learning is achieved through the visual stimuli. When visual aids are added to aural instruction, 35 percent more information can be absorbed in the same time and retention of information is about 55 percent better.[3]

VISUALS HELP THE AUDIENCE AND THE SPEAKER

Visual aids are virtually indispensible to the business communicator. They serve at least four important functions:

1. They help crystalize vague or abstract ideas in the minds of your listeners.
2. They help your listeners retain information—illustrated ideas linger in the mind.
3. They help you fight the speaker's enemies: listener boredom, daydreaming, confusion, and apathy.
4. They serve as guides to keep the speaker on track—in effect they can be your notes.

Let's talk for a moment about how visuals help you as the speaker. Visuals should be recognized as an integral part of your presentation, not an afterthought to be tacked on. When this is so, visuals can help you in three phases of your presentation: conceptual planning, developing the content of your talk, and delivering your message.

In conceptual planning, thinking about visuals you might use can spark creative ideas and enthusiasm for the project. You might consider places where visuals will fit using the "TIMM'S CAT" memory aid we discussed in Chapter 2. Visuals may fit nicely into virtually any of the eight steps from statements of *topic* to selection of *take-home* materials.

As you develop the content of your message, visuals can help in the organizing of ideas, strengthening the impact of the message, creating continuity of thought, providing variety for your listeners, and clarifying important concepts or associations.

Finally, visuals help you in delivery by providing an outline of key thoughts, increasing your self-confidence, permitting spontaneous action and movement, and diverting attention from the speaker and toward the message. The overall result is an improved audience impression of you as a speaker.

In the following pages I'll discuss three classes of visual aids and offer suggestions for effective use of each. The three types are *direct* visuals, *projected* visuals, and *dynamic* visuals. The emphasis will be on the kinds of visuals the business speaker can readily use without calling for elaborate specialized professional preparation. The important point is that to be effective communicators we must use some visual support materials.

DIRECT VISUALS

Direct visuals can range from the very simple flip chart or chalkboard, to the more sophisticated three dimensional model or mock-up. Probably the single most important thing to remember about the direct visual is to keep it *simple and concise*. This is especially true of graphs, charts, or other illustrations. Simple illustrations need not be unattractive or ineffective. In fact, often the simple design lingers in the mind of the receiver very effectively.

Here are some simple types of direct visuals and suggestions as to how they can be made.

Word charts. A word chart is probably your simplest visual aide. In preparing word charts, economy of language is crucial. Be sure that the lettering is large so that everyone in your audience can read it. The sample chart illustrated in Figure 9-1 shows you some rules for making word charts for your presentation.

```
┌─────────────────────────────────────┐
│            SAMPLEWOOD                │
│              CHART                   │
├─────────────────────────────────────┤
│  1.  Keep It Simple                  │
│  2.  Use Only 5 or 6 Lines of Print  │
│  3.  List Only Key Points            │
│  4.  Make the Lettering Large        │
│  5.  Use Exact Phrasing              │
└─────────────────────────────────────┘
```

FIGURE 9-1
Word chart

When using word charts, we need not always be limited to posterboard mounted on a tripod. One alternative is to make boxes or three-sided charts that stand alone. On each side of the visual is a different word chart. Other sets of word charts or simple graphs can be stacked inside each other and removed as needed. This approach has the added advantage of avoiding the common problem of charts that slip off the tripod or fall off the wall. These 3-dimensional charts can be placed on a table or the floor (if your listeners can see them there) as you speak. The added advantage is that they are different from the visuals most people have come to expect, so they hold attention better.

Pie charts. A pie chart is a simple, circular illustration that is divided into segments to show part-to-whole comparisons. It can effectively show only a few broad divisions. If you use a pie chart, remember these things:

1. Cut the segments of the pie accurately, usually beginning at the top and moving clockwise for each new segment.
2. Label each "slice," showing what it represents and the percentage it represents.
3. Use large, clear lettering for the chart; Such a chart is shown in Figure 9-2.

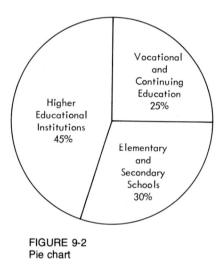

FIGURE 9-2
Pie chart

Line, Bar, and Column Graphs. A line graph gives a continuous picture showing trends or changes over time as shown in Figure 9-3. It can also show simple comparisons of trends as in Figure 9-4. Avoid having too many lines on the chart. Color coding can be helpful to clarify the message.

If you'll look back at Figure 9-3, I'd like to point out a potential problem with line graphs. A quick glance at these two graphs conveys information which could be misleading to the viewer. The drop in the value of the dollar appears to be as great as the increase in the price of gold. A more careful look at percentage changes, however, tells a different story. Gold went from around $200 per ounce to $360 (a 180 percent increase) while dollar value went from around $.50 to $.45 (a 10 percent decrease). The different scales on the vertical axis of the graph suggest a more dramatic change than actually occurred. If these two graphs were displayed together, implying a comparison, a misleading conclusion may be reached by the viewer. The data are distorted.

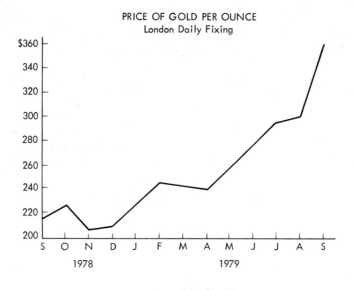

PRICE OF GOLD PER OUNCE
London Daily Fixing

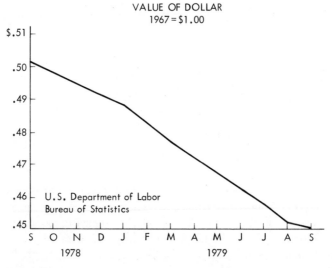

VALUE OF DOLLAR
1967 = $1.00

U.S. Department of Labor
Bureau of Statistics

FIGURE 9-3
Line graphs

The bar or column graph can quickly show comparative magnitudes of quantities. The bar graph uses a horizontal design while columns are vertical. Figure 9-5 shows a column graph.

Dry Mounted Pictures. Photographs or drawings can provide excellent visual support. If you have photos or pictures large enough for a presentation,

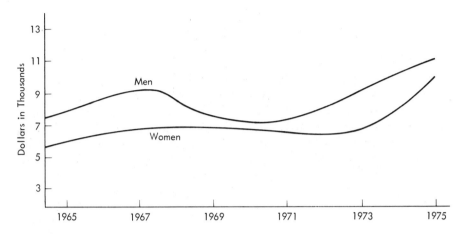

FIGURE 9-4
Line graph showing comparison of trends

their usefulness may be hampered by their large size and light-weight paper. They become awkward to handle and lack durability.

One simple and relatively inexpensive technique for overcoming these disadvantages is *dry-mounting*. "Dry-mounting adheres display material to backings such as posterboard or masonite. There is no messy paste or glue involved in the process. Dry-mounting tissue is placed between the visual and the backing material. This tissue is a thin sheet of rice paper coated on both sides with a heat sensitive adhesive. Once heat is applied, the adhesive softens and adheres the visual to the backing posterboard or other material."[4]

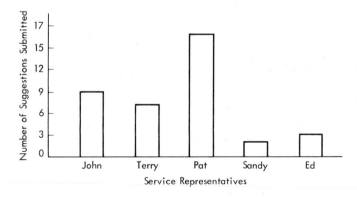

FIGURE 9-5
Column graph

Almost any type direct visual can be dry-mounted. The only equipment necessary is a dry-mount press, a tacking iron, a metal edged ruler and a cutting knife. Such equipment will give many years of service.[5]

Dry-mounting adds professionalism as well as durability to visuals and sure beats fumbling with flimsy photos or paper illustrations.

Props or Models. When your audience is relatively small, you may want to use props or models. A nuclear reactor engineer used a prop to gain audience attention this way. Holding up a small segment of a nuclear fuel element, he surprised (and got the attention of) his audience with this statement: "This small piece of atomic fuel weighs a little over two pounds, yet it is capable of generating the heat equivalent of over two thousand tons of coal."

When giving a talk to explain the workings of a new machine, it obviously makes sense to have the machine there as a prop.

As a rule, don't pass around models or props. Your listeners will become former listeners as they focus attention on the object you've given them to play with.

New Ideas in Direct Visuals. A number of variations of direct visual displays have become available in recent years. Chalkboards are being replaced by lighter-colored "liquid chalkboards." Here, the speaker draws with felt-tip pens (in multi-colors) which erase easily. Another recent innovation is the "Hook N' Loop*" presentation boards. These use a fabric coating on the display board and a special hook tape which attaches to the back of anything you want to put on the board. The big advantage here is that 3-dimensional objects (including plastic letters and symbols available through the manufacturers) can be displayed. The effect is very professional.

MAKING THE BEST OF DIRECT VISUALS

Direct visuals are generally inexpensive and very appropriate to most business presentations. When designing and using them, remember these key rules.

1. Keep them *simple.*
2. Keep them *clear.* (Use different colors, etc. to highlight key information.)
3. Place the visual where it can be seen by everyone. (Don't stand in front of it as you explain the material.)
4. Don't talk to the visual aid; maintain eye contact with your listeners.
5. Display the visual only when it is in use. (Showing it too early or, in some cases, leaving it up too long, can be distracting.)

*Hook N' Loop is a registered trademark of Mayer Presentation Systems, 168 East Market Street, Akron, OH 44308

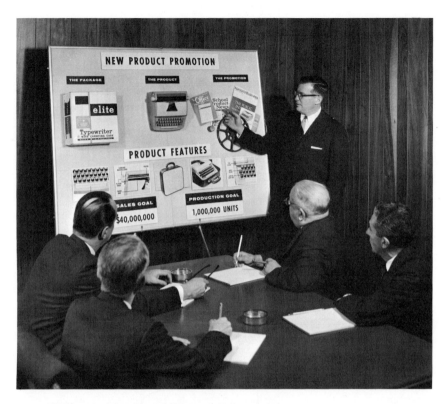

Source: Charles Mayer Studios, Inc. Reprinted by permission.

6. Use visuals only to support important ideas in your presentation. (The time and effort of creating visuals conveys to your audience that this aspect of your talk is very important. Make sure it really is.)
7. Strive for professionalism in the design of your visuals. Get artistic help when necessary. (Your visuals *do* reflect on your credibility too.)

BADLY USED VISUALS: AN OCCUPATIONAL DISEASE

Harry E. Hand discusses the misuse of visuals calling it an "occupational disease." In an entertaining way, he talks about a fictitious professor named Whiffle:[6]

> The habit of badly using bad visual aids is rampant among those who "speak to inform." It is an occupational disease of university professors. Severe epidemics

break out at every scientific, engineering, and medical convention. Someone has said that the hoof-and-mouth disease sometimes spreads to other species; and when it does, it is often complicated by a heavy incidence of Whiffle's syndrome.

Whiffle is an organic chemist. He became so famous for his researches that every chemists' club wanted him to come and tell them the story. At the first few meetings of this kind, he just spoke. Then it occurred to him that diagrams of some of his big organic molecules would look impressive, so he had some slides made. In the slides, each atom in the molecule was shown by means of a small circle; lines connecting the circles showed how they were bonded together. That was fine at first, but as his research continued, he developed bigger and bigger molecules. To get them on a lantern slide, he had to make the scale of the drawings smaller and smaller. By the time the molecules got up to a few thousand atoms, the circles got so small that they looked like the dots of a halftone engraving. Whiffle thought the slides seemed a trifle crowded, but he was busy, so he has been using them ever since.

Whiffle also wanted to show some of the smaller molecules in three dimensions. He couldn't do this on the screen, so he built cagelike models of the molecules out of wooden balls and stiff wire. With the balls and wire painted in different colors to represent different kinds of atoms and bonds, they were very impressive, although it must be admitted that Whiffle displayed them more as a curiosity than as vital, concrete support for his talk. The audiences always duly admired the workmanship, but only one person ever asked any questions about the models. That was the young son of one presiding officer who brought the boy along when the baby-sitter failed to show up. The boy's question was whether Whiffle didn't think they would make good cages for squirrels.

As time went on, other symptoms began to appear in Whiffle's talks—such as standing in front of what he had written on the blackboard, or passing around so many specimens that half the people in the audience would be busy handling them. Those readers who wish to investigate the full array of symptoms included in Whiffle's syndrome are referred to the exhaustive descriptions that have appeared in the journals devoted to abnormal psychology. Briefly, the symptoms all stem from Whiffle's apparent belief that visual aids automatically ensure interest, understanding, and conviction.

PROJECTED VISUALS: "WILL SOMEBODY GET THE LIGHTS, PLEASE?"

The two most prominent projected visuals are the overhead transparency and slides.

These have two major advantages over direct visuals.

1. They are less cumbersome to use, and
2. They can be used with large audiences which may not be able to see direct visuals.

Overhead transparencies. Perhaps the simplest projected visual to use is the overhead transparency. Today's transparency projectors are often portable, quiet, and capable of reproducing a very sharp image. The transparencies themselves can be made very simply often using a xerographic copy as a master. This enables the presenter to get cartoons, newspaper clippings, line drawings, and illustrations of many different types and quickly convert them into overhead transparencies. In addition, felt tip pens especially for writing on transparencies are readily available. These permit the speaker to put a transparency on display, and then add to it in his own handwriting. Or, in situations where a chalkboard or flip chart are not available, a presenter can simply write out key ideas on a blank transparency sheet as he speaks. This would then be projected on a wall or screen for easy viewing by the audience. This has the added benefit of allowing the speaker to maintain eye contact while continuing to face the audience as he or she writes on the transparency. I have used this quite extensively in recent months and have found it to be very useful.

Another use for the overhead transparency projector I've found especially enjoyable is the display of *cartoons*. Cartoons can frequently convey in very few words an important concept or idea. Cartoonists often use stock symbols to communicate messages rapidly without too much detail. It is a simple process to make overhead transparencies of cartoons you have clipped from newspapers or magazines. These can add a great deal to your presentation if they fit into the flow of thought. In this book I've attempted to use some selected cartoons to emphasize key communication ideas. The same principle applies in oral presentations.

Slides. Photographic slides can be produced very inexpensively and can provide a very professional image to your presentation. There are at least three sources of good slides. First, the speaker or his or her staff can take precisely the slides needed for the planned presentation. Second, photographic slides can be purchased or shot-to-order by a professional photographer. A third option is to turn to professionals who prepare slides using computer technology. An organization called Chartmasters, Inc. produces an extremely high quality slide for professional presentations. The equipment used by this corporation is called Genigraphics.* It works this way: Working at a typewriter like a keyboard, the artist keys your data into the system's computer. He designs formats or retrieves them from the computer's memory bank. He plots data points, changes copy sizes, composes, recomposes, and illustrates. He can render over 8 million colors in otherwise impossible juxtapositions, giving the slide the communications impact required. As these elements are integrated, they are instantly displayed on a television screen for the artist's approval. During this creative process, the artist can change the colors and other elements as desired.

Illustrations of several Chartmaster slides are presented in Figure 9-6.

MAKING THE BEST OF PROJECTED VISUALS

Here are some suggestions for maximizing your effectiveness with projected visuals:

*Genigraphics is a trademark of the General Electric Corporation.

1. Use simple slides. Slides are especially useful in showing entire structures or complicated pieces of equipment or for the comparison of data such as graphs, charts and so forth. Their judicious use can greatly enhance the value and understanding of a talk. But remember, the slides are used to supplement your business presentation not vice versa. Don't let your talk become a commentary on your slides.

2. Leave the lights on while you show the slides. This is probably the easiest remedy for the worst drawback to the use of slides. Most slides if properly prepared, can be seen with normal projection equipment if the lights in the room are still kept at normal strength or slightly dimmed. By keeping the room lighted you avoid the problem of losing listeners who tend to doze off in the semi-darkness. You maintain eye contact with them more effectively and you'll be able to see and talk with them as individuals rather than as some amorphous mass somewhere beyond you in the dark.

3. Use the type of slide equipment that permits you to avoid running back and forth to the slide projector. Most modern slide projectors have a remote control device which allows you to change the slide without physically touching the projector. This is most desirable. With overhead transparencies, however, this cannot be done. When showing transparencies, the effective presenter will strive to be as unobtrusive as possible. Don't stop in the middle of a thought or line of reasoning and abruptly change the visual. When preparing for your presentation think about when these transparencies must be changed, then strive to do so smoothly and with minimal distraction to your audience.

4. Don't turn away from your audience and talk to the image on the screen. This is a particular problem when speaking to a larger group and using a microphone. Each time a new image appears on the screen, some speakers turn towards that image and away from the microphone causing their voice to fade.

5. Finally, keep your slides to a reasonable number. Slides should not be used to give a complete outline of your talk, to present the intricacies of mathematical derivations, or to present a wealth of complex test data. If the details of complicated test data are significant and important for your audience to understand they should be given a hard copy to take along. A quick look may be more frustrating then informative. A bunch of equations thrown at an audience which is unfamiliar with them is a waste of time.

The abrupt shift from one slide to the next is another possible distraction which can be eliminated. Try using two projectors in electronic parallel and hook-up so that instead of changing slides on one machine, the first slide fades out (as the lamp is turned off) while the second slide fades in (as its lamp is turned on). While the lamp is off, machine number one advances to the next

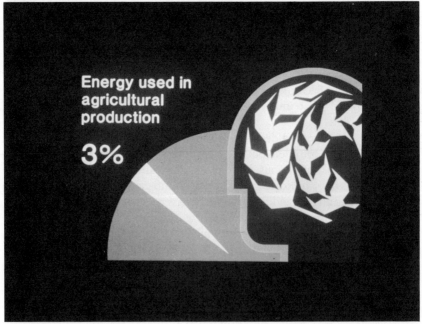

FIGURE 9-6

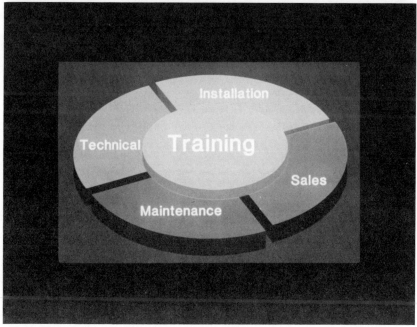

FIGURE 9-6 (cont.)

Direct or projected visuals should simplify the message for your listeners.

slide, ready to turn back on when machine number two shuts off. (Your photo supply dealer can explain how to make this hook-up.) The effect is very professional and smooth. Coordinating this with a tape recorded message and inaudible "beeps" to signal slide advance can make for a classy presentation. This would be worth setting up for presentations which will be given repeatedly such as new employee orientations or public relations displays.

Projected visuals are valuable when used with discretion. They work best when we observe these rules:

1. Attempt to convey only one idea with clarity. Exclude irrelevant information.
2. Remove unnecessary detail to keep subject matter simple.
3. Limit words or numbers to 15 or 20 at the very most. Make them large enough to be clearly visible to all viewers.
4. Avoid complex tables. Chart or graph format is much clearer.
5. Use color for visual attractiveness and emphasis.
6. Use several different slides to convey complicated ideas.

DYNAMIC VISUALS

A dynamic visual shows motion and sound. The most common types are movies and video tapes.

Traditionally the cost of producing dynamic visuals has been high. But that is changing rapidly. Movies with sound can now be shot at low cost using the newer generation of "home movie" equipment. "Instant" movies such as those produced by Polaroid products are available. But in my opinion, the videotape holds the most promise for business speakers.

Videotapes can be produced almost as easily as an audio tape. Videocassettes are easy to store and play back—again, as easy as a standard tape recorder. And the cost of equipment is very reasonable.

Dynamic visuals can be especially useful in training situations. I've had considerable success in using videotapes in communication training workshops. Participants in role-play situations ranging from presentational speaking to performance appraisals can benefit from an objective view of themselves in action. It can be a real eye-opener.

A FINAL THOUGHT ABOUT AUDIO-VISUAL AIDS: CHECK OUT IN ADVANCE

No discussion of visual/audio aids can be complete without mentioning the importance of pre-presentation planning. We've all been at presentations where the gremlins inside the microphone or projector caused something to go dead or burn out. It is crucial for you as a speaker to be as well prepared as possible for such problems. Be sure to arrive early enough to test equipment. Bring spare projector bulbs. Check out the videotape player or movie projector. Do everything possible to prepare for possible problems. Have contingency plans if all else fails.

Visual/audio aids can be a terrific boost to your presentation. They can also, on occasion, distract or even destroy a talk. Nonetheless, I strongly recommend their usage. Consider the points in this chapter as you prepare to use visuals and you'll be likely to avoid the pitfalls they can provide.

Figure 9-7 presents a summary of visual and audio aids.[7] Although the classifications are slightly different from mine, this description of advantages and disadvantages is excellent.

The following table is a summary of the various kinds of visual and audio aids, including their advantages and disadvantages.

FIGURE 9-7
Summary of visual and audio aids: advantages and disadvantages

Visual Aid	*Advantages*	*Disadvantages*
	Direct Visuals	
Gestures and bodily movement	Spontaneous Add animation to report	Limited to fairly simple ideas
Three-dimensional materials		
Objects	Authentic Realistic	May offer only a limited view May be too large or too small

Visual Aid	Advantages	Disadvantages
Models	May be better adapted in size than objects May reveal inner features	May be too bulky to be easily stored or transported Not suitable for large audience May not be available May be expensive or time-consuming to secure Not suitable for large audience
Mock-ups	Focus on essential features	Same as for models
Pictures	Little if any expense Show pictorial realism	Suitable for very small audiences Difficult to hold and point out features at same time
Handouts	May be seen by everyone May be retained for future reference	Loss of control over listener attention
Chalkboard	Usually available Permits spontaneity in use Useful for visuals requiring little preparation Useful for adding to ideas	Not suitable for complicated diagrams, etc. Tends to reduce contact with audience Erasures appear smudgy Material cannot be readily saved Cannot be transported
Charts	Allow more contact with audience than most visuals Can be prepared in advance Can be made very attractive Simple to set up and manage Pencil notes can be placed on charts Easily referred to later in report Can be stored and transported if necessary	Not effective with large audiences Not useful for pictorial realism May require much preparation time Not as easy to add material to as the chalkboard or overhead projection More limited work area than chalkboard Comparatively bulky to store or transport
Flannel board	Visuals prepared ahead of time Allows progressive buildup of idea Can accommodate three-dimensional visuals Helps speaker remember pattern of report	Not effective with large audiences Bulky to transport

Graphs

Graphs (general)	More interesting than tables Bring out comparisons and	Generally less complete and accurate than tables

Visual Aid	Advantages	Disadvantages
	trends more clearly than tables Convey the gist of the data more quickly than tables	
Circle graphs	Ideal for showing parts of a whole	
Line graphs	Ideal for showing trends or variations over a period of time	
Bar graphs	Ideal for showing comparisons Easiest to grasp at a glance	
Pictorial graphs	More eye-appealing than other graphs	Less accurate to read More difficult to prepare

Projected Visuals

Visual Aid	Advantages	Disadvantages
Projections (general)	*Only* visual suited for large audience Can portray pictorial realism Usually professional looking Simple to store or transport	Numerous mechanics involved in operation Tend to usurp role of speaker
2- by 2-in. projections	Superior for photographs Can be operated by speaker through remote control Comparatively inexpensive Easy to store or transport	Require a day or two for processing May involve some waste of film
3¼- by 4-in. projections	Can be "do it yourself" Can utilize Polaroid instant transparencies Larger work area than on 2- by 2-in. slides	Slides and projector both bulkier than 2- by 2-in. to handle, store, or transport Slides and projector both more expensive than 2- by 2-in. Projector no longer as common as 2- by 2-in. Cannot be operated by remote control Room ordinarily darker than with 2- by 2-in.
Overhead projections	Room need not be darkened Speaker can face audience Transparencies simple to prepare Transparencies inexpensive to prepare Professional results obtainable in transparencies	Keystone effect on screen Projector tends to obstruct audience view Projector bulky to store and usually too bulky to transport

FIGURE 9-7. Summary of visual and audio aids: advantages and disadvantages (cont.)

Visual Aid	Advantages	Disadvantages
	Easy to add or remove details	
	Easy to point out details while facing audience	
	Animation effect can be created	
	Pencil notations can be made on frames	
	Transparencies easy to store or transport	
Microprojections	Show magnifications	Not useful for other kinds of projections
Motion-picture projections	Show motion	Expensive to prepare Require trained operator
Closed-circuit television (CCTV) (with video-tape)	Shows motion No delay for processing No cost for processing Allows spontaneity in use Useful for trial and error in developing visuals Useful for rehearsal	Requires trained operator Not useful outside studio Small "projection" screen Shows image only in black and white Equipment is expensive
Opaque projections	No processing necessary to produce projections	Speaker usually cannot face audience unless he has a projectionist Projector tends to block audience view Projector blower comparatively noisy Strong light may "blind" audience when projection stage is lowered

Audio Aids

Tape recorder	Usually portable Tape may be reused indefinitely Permits alteration of sounds for analysis Permits perfection of sound materials Permits exact timing	
Disc recorder		Cannot be taken to source of sound Discs not reusable

VISUAL AIDS: SHARPEN KEY POINTS, FOCUS THE PICTURE

Chapter 9. A summary of key ideas

1. Since most people have difficulty visualizing from the spoken word alone (we are of the TV generation), visual aids are necessary in almost any oral presentation.
2. Listener comprehension and retention of the message can increase significantly when visual aids are used to support ideas.
3. Visuals help both the speaker and the audience.
   (a) In conceptual planning they can spark creative ideas and create enthusiasm.
   (b) In developing content they can help organize ideas, create continuity, and strengthen the impact of the message.
   (c) In delivery they provide an outline of key thoughts, increase self-confidence and permit spontaneous action and movement.
   (d) For listeners they provide variety, interest, and clarification.
4. Direct visuals can range from the very simple chalkboard or flipchart to the more complex working models. Common types of direct visuals are
   (a) word charts
   (b) pie charts
   (c) line, bar and column graphs
   (d) dry mounted pictures
   (e) props or models
   (f) presentation boards.
5. Projected visuals such as transparencies and slides are less cumbersome than direct visuals and are more acceptable to larger audiences.
6. Dynamic visuals such as movies and videotapes are useful in extended presentations or training sessions. Their costs are coming down fast with new technology.
7. Always check out the use of audio/visual equipment in advance. Be prepared for such common problems as burned out bulbs.

NOTES

1. Conwell Carlson. "Best Memories by Eye and the Ear," *The Kansas City Times* (April 19, 1967), p. 13A.
2. Robert L. Montgomery. *A Master Guide to Public Speaking* (New York: Harper and Row, Pub., 1979), p. 36.

3. Stephen S. Pride. *Business Ideas: How To Create and Present Them* (New York: Harper and Row, Pub., 1967), p. 172.

4. James J. Kenny, "Don't Overlook Simple Graphics," *Training, 16,* 4, (April 1979).

5. Ibid.

6. From EFFECTIVE SPEAKING FOR THE TECHNICAL MAN by Harry E. Hand (c) 1969 by Litton Educational Publishing, Inc. Reprinted by permission of Van Nostrand Reinhold Company.

7. From James W. Brown, et. al., A-V INSTRUCTION MATERIALS AND METHODS, pp. 317–318 (1959). Reprinted by permission of McGraw-Hill Book Company.

10

DELIVERING THE PRESENTATION

OBJECTIVES OF CHAPTER 10

After studying this chapter, the reader should be able to

1. Name and give examples of six classes of nonverbal variables which can affect the speaker's "total image."
2. Identify six common mistakes which can nonverbally detract from the speaker's message.
3. Describe the five aspects of voice and paralanguage which affect delivery.
4. Explain the advantages and disadvantages of notes versus a manuscript.
5. Describe eight techniques for maximizing the question-answer approach to listener participation.

No matter how much work you've done on your presentation up to this point your success will still depend in large part on the way your talk is delivered. It is only through the use of body and voice that our presentation becomes a reality.

This chapter will be divided into two general sections. First we will consider *personal characteristics* which affect the way we deliver a talk. Each of us projects a "total image" as we communicate with others. We will consider some of the factors that make up this total image in the first part of this chapter. The second general area to be considered in this chapter might be called *"procedural considerations in delivery."* Here we will talk about using notes or manuscripts, handling questions and answers, and generating participative responses from our listeners.

PERSONAL CHARACTERISTICS AFFECTING DELIVERY

I said a moment ago that each of us projects a total image as we communicate with others. Anything we do or say (or don't do, or don't say!) can conceivably be interpreted by others as having some meaning. Much of this image is conveyed nonverbally, that is, without the use of words. Nonverbal variables have tremendous impact on our communication effectiveness. The extent to which we are able to control them, or at least take them into account as we deliver verbal messages, is the extent to which we will be successful communicators.

In the business context there are six classes of nonverbal variables which we should be aware of:

1. Personal space
2. Appearance
3. Body movements
4. Touching behaviors
5. Facial expression and eye contact
6. Vocal cues and paralanguage.

Our sensitivity to these variables and the ways we use them (or fail to use them) largely create our speaking image. Let's talk briefly about each.

Personal space and speaking position. Researchers in nonverbal communication find that there are certain expectations about how far or how close to others we should position ourselves in given communication situations. The distance of less than 18 inches is reserved for intimate communication or conspiracies. Normal conversational communication takes place at about two to four feet; we remain at arms length. At meetings and conferences, we feel comfortable at a distance of 4 to 12 feet from the individuals we are speaking with. Beyond 12 feet is generally reserved for public speech. The point here is that there are certain social/cultural expectations that our listeners have. If we violate these normal space patterns, we may confuse or distract our listener. For example, the speaker in a briefing who moves in too close to some of his listeners, may make them quite uncomfortable. By the same token, the speaker who stands back too far may come across as being aloof. We need to be sensitive to what people regard as normal. It can be especially dangerous to invade someone's "personal bubble."

A business acquaintance of mine had the annoying habit of standing too close to other people when talking. The problem was compounded by the fact that he was quite tall. The impression he conveyed was one of dominance which was uncomfortable to others.

Appearance. Our personal appearance creates an initial impression that is sometimes very powerful. The way we dress, the way we groom ourselves, our posture or bearing, all lend themselves to the total impression that we give to our audience. One area where we have considerable control is over our selection of clothing. The clothes we wear should be appropriate to the occasion. They should not be so out of the ordinary that they draw our listener's attention away from our intended message. Attractive dress can play an important role in influencing others. Generally, perceived attractiveness will increase the credibility of the speaker and possibly give him or her a persuasive advantage over a less attractive person.

Body movement and gestures. Our personal dynamism or self-confidence, which you recall is one dimension of credibility, comes across by

FUNNY BUSINESS   by Roger Bollen

What we wear should not distract our listeners from what we are saying.

way of such body language as gestures, posture, and mannerisms. There are a number of types of gestures of course, including facial expressions, hand movements, and body positioning. Gestures can be particularly useful to punctuate what has been said. They should, however, be spontaneous and natural, yet purposeful. We all have different tendencies to use or avoid gestures. For some, it feels uncomfortable to point or raise hands in exclamation. For others it may be said that if you tied their hands they would be speechless. In my experience, few people overuse gestures. Some, however, fail to take advantage of the sense of movement or enthusiasm that gestures can provide.

There are several common mistakes people make with gestures. (1) They fail to use them where they can be very useful for emphasis. (2) They fail to use a variety of gestures. The same gesture over and over becomes monotonous or even distracting. (3) They use gestures that cannot be seen clearly; a hand motion obstructed from audience view by a podium, for example, is of no value.

Effective gestures are both purposeful and natural. Nervous gestures, such as those of the speaker who persistently adjusts his tie, scratches an ear, or adjusts his or her hairdo, may feel natural, but are not purposeful. These can be distracting or even infuriating to the audience. If you suspect that you are guilty of distracting nervous gestures, ask a trusted associate to give you some candid feedback after your presentation. Being aware of these things can help reduce the problem.

For the person who feels uncomfortable using hand gestures, I suggest this: Force yourself to try out some hand movements as you speak. One simple form of gesture, which audiences commonly expect from speakers, is the holding up of the hand when you are enumerating key points. For example, if you reach a point in your talk where you are listing three reasons for something, hold up one finger for the first, two for the second, and so forth. Although even this may feel awkward to some speakers, it's important that we experiment with behaviors to see what our listener reactions will be. Eventually, the use of gestures, can become very normal and comfortable.

Body movement is another very important way to bring life to a talk. Your pausing between key points in the briefing and physically moving to another place in the room will help your audience to know that you have completed one point and are now ready to address another. In this sense, it is like a nonverbal transition. This pause helps your listener follow the logical development of what you have to say. If you cannot freely move around because you must speak into a microphone, you may still use the pause and shift in position, or change in the direction in which you are looking to indicate the same things. Physical movement is the preferred approach. Whenever possible, avoid the speaker-behind-the-podium format. If a microphone is needed, a portable mike around the neck will allow you more freedom of movement. As one writer has said, "Move, and the world moves with you; stand, and you stand alone."

Touching behaviors. Mark L. Knapp, an expert in nonverbal communication, suggests that touching behavior can convey very different information depending upon the participants and context in which it occurs. Generally he sees touch as "a crucial aspect of most human relationships. It plays a part in giving encouragement, expressing tenderness, showing emotional support, and many other things."[1] He also suggests that physical contact is a way of breaking through some psychological barriers between people.

For the business speaker, touching the audience (physically, that is) may be difficult, inappropriate or awkward. Nevertheless, on occasions where the number of listeners is few, a speaker can convey enthusiasm, sincerity, or simply a liking for others with a warm handshake or a sincere pat on the back. But be careful not to overdo it. Some people recoil at any prolonged touch. A brief handshake or back-pat is acceptable to almost anyone in our culture but extended hand-holding or stroking may make another person very uncomfortable. Appropriate touching can communicate important information (such as liking, enthusiasm, sincerity, and so forth). But inappropriate or excessive touching can damage credibility and put your listeners in an awkward position.

Facial expression and eye contact. Your face and eyes tend to be the focus for your listeners as you speak. The face can convey enthusiasm, anger, sincerity, and many other feelings. In short, your facial expression will almost always express how you *feel* about what you are saying.

Perhaps the single most important part of the face is the eyes. Most of us have learned never to trust a person who won't look us in the eye. It's a cultural expectation that when people communicate with each other they look at each other. The shifty-eyed individual, who refuses to look at you when communicating, is widely distrusted. Conversely the individual who seems to pierce through us with an unwavering stare, makes us very uncomfortable. I recall a recent political advertisement on television where the candidate stared directly into the camera, unflinchingly. Although he appeared to be communicating with the television viewer, it was uncomfortable to watch him. Researchers have found generally that people are most comfortable with someone who looks at them, but who occasionally blinks or looks away for a moment.

Research on eye contact indicates that we establish and maintain eye contact under these conditions:

1.   When we are seeking feedback concerning the reactions of others.
2.   When we want to signal that the communication channel is open.
3.   When we want to convey our need for affiliation, involvement, or inclusion with the group to whom we are speaking.

The absence of eye contact tends to convey quite different messages:

1.   We want to hide something.
2.   There is dislike or tension between participants in the communication situation.
3.   A recent deception or lie has been told.
4.   The individual wishes to disavow a social relationship with others in the communication situation.
5.   The speaker is about to begin a long utterance.

With the exception of number five, the absence of eye contact expresses a desire to avoid communicating. The presence of eye contact, on the other hand, conveys a desire to create better understanding.

When addressing a larger group, maintaining eye contact can become a problem. The best bet seems to be to look at one individual for a few seconds then move on to another. Don't just scan the crowd—really look *at* individuals. Be sure you get to almost everyone in the room at some point. Be aware of tendencies to look too much at one particularly attractive person while ignoring the ugly guy at the back of the room. Look at people randomly; that is, don't persistently scan from left to right or front to rear as though you were programmed to do so. Also, do not simply look over the heads of your audience and fix your gaze on something or someone behind them.

Ideally in presentational speaking, you can establish and maintain eye contact similar to what you would do in a face-to-face, one-to-one conversation. The size of your audience, of course, makes such contact momentary rather than consistent as you speak.

Vocal cues and paralanguage. * The way we say things can strengthen or even contradict what we say. A simple example is the man or woman who is obviously enraged (as expressed by nonverbal cues) who shouts, "I am not angry!" Or the half-hearted expression of support from a co-worker who says, "Yeah, that'll be swell." Again, vocal characteristics are a part of the total image projected nonverbally. Let's consider several aspects of voice and paralanguage: articulation, pronunciation, voice quality, verbalized pauses, and emphasis.

Articulation. Speech scientists distinguish between voice and articulation in this way: Voice is the *sound* while articulation is the manipulation of that sound into phonemes and words by use of the tongue, lips, jaw, and so forth. The sounds of the English language cannot be articulated clearly through half-closed lips. Get the jaw moving—it's hinged so that you can— to avoid common articulation problems. Among the more frequent of these problems are

Omitting final consonants (goin instead of go*ing;* havin instead of hav*ing;* ya instead of you)

Omitting other sounds (liberry instead of lib*ra*ry; tempature instead of temperature)

Inserting additional sounds (ath*a*lete instead of athlete)

Distorting sounds (crick instead of creek; flusterated instead of frustrated)

---

*Paralanguage refers to *how* something is said and not *what* is said.

Your articulation should be precise but not artificial sounding. Be natural but be correct.

Pronunciation. Being careful not to mispronounce words may be more important than you think. As with other distractions, such goofs may not seriously change meaning but will reflect on your credibility. I have heard data processing people mispronounce statistics as "satistics" and supervisors explain "pacific" examples. Recently I heard a professor commenting about the unusually rainy weather we've been having. He hoped that the "moon-san" season was soon to end. I think he meant monsoon. While at an Air Force training school I was surprised to hear that "humid air" is responsible for a number of plane crashes. Finally, I saw this culprit described in writing. It was "human error."

Few things can distract listeners more quickly than a badly mispronounced word. When you are unclear about the correct pronunciation, there are several sources you might consult. Although the dictionary is frequently recommended, ocassionally regional or local differences in pronunciation make even the dictionary version sound awkward to specific audiences. The best bet is to determine how a term is normally used locally by asking others and by listening carefully.

Voice qualities. A speaker's voice reflects his or her personality. A clear, strong voice increases the probability of audience understanding. Other voice characteristics such as variation in pitch, loudness, and rate of speech are important in gaining and holding listener interest. The range of pitch may be wide, allowing for effective vocal emphasis, or very narrow, resulting in what is commonly called a monotone. Over time, a committed monotone can, as the sleeping aid commercial says, "Help you relax, feel drowsy so you can fall asleep."

A key word to keeping listener attention is *variation*. Psychologist William James tells us that, "No one can possibly attend continuously to an object that does not change." From my experience in coaching speakers, there are two very common voice variation problems that come up over and over again. For many male speakers, there is seldom enough variation in pitch. Men seem to think that it sounds "macho" to talk only in a deep tone and they do so continuously. Ted Baxter, the obnoxious newscaster on the old Mary Tyler Moore Show, is a classic example of this. His persistent use of the stage voice, presumably to sound emphatic and masculine, got many laughs on the program. In real life, the speaker with a Ted Baxter voice would be perceived as very phoney at best.

Tremendous emphasis can be made by raising and lowering the pitch, yet many speakers do not want to "risk" it. Nevertheless, if we listen to particularly successful radio or television announcers, comedians, or other entertainers, we will find that they do in fact vary the pitch of their voices significantly. It is almost impossible to develop effective emphasis techniques without varying pitch. I'd strongly encourage you to try some different behaviors with your voice. Try going a little higher or a little lower or simply adding a little more variation to your voice as you speak. I think you will find your listeners' reactions will be positive.

One of the more prominent difficulties that I've seen among some female speakers is that they tend to lose the conversational tone in their voices when they address a group. The voice tends to sound theatrical or artificial. Occasionally this comes out "sing-songy." This problem results from habitual pitch change patterns that become monotonous and distracting. It also arises from overdoing voice intensity, perhaps in an effort to sound more assertive. We've all experienced people who are overly loud as well as some who are so soft-spoken, we want to ask them to speak up. Most business presentations can be made in a normal conversational level of intensity although additional emphasis may be achieved by variations in loudness. Don't assume always that the louder voice commands more attention. Often that soft-spoken voice—the one we have to lean toward and work to hear—is the most powerful.

One further point about voice pitch. Some people have the rather distracting habit of raising the pitch of their last words to convey a questioning tone at the end of a statement. This can confuse an audience and convey an impression of your being uncertain about your ideas. Try to become sensitive to this if it is a problem for you.

Verbalized pauses. Few things can drive your audience up a wall like the liberal use of "ah," "um," "uh," and the popular "ya know." I have heard intelligent and apparently rational men and women salt their every utterance with these expressions till I want to scream at them, ya know?

The human talker abhors a vacuum. And when the detested monster, silence, raises its ugly head we beat it to death with ah, uh, um, or ya know's.

Perhaps the first step in eliminating these highly distracting nonfluen-

Vocal variation creates enthusiasm—which can be contagious.

cies from your speech is to rid yourself of the fear of silence. Often a pause or hesitation in speech can convey a sense of deliberateness, care in preparation, and even emphasis on key points. In fact, many would contend that a pause is one of your most effective types of emphasis. Don't fill it up by verbalizing some meaningless expression.

Do yourself a favor; ask a trusted associate you speak with to point out when you are drifting into the habit of verbalizing pauses.

Emphasis. Putting more impact behind certain words can have interesting effects on meaning. Think of the different ways you can emphasize the question "What do you mean by that?"

What do you mean by that?

What *do* you mean by that?

What do *you* mean by that?

What do you *mean* by that?

What do you mean by *that?*

Professional communicators are very sensitive to these kinds of differences. Listen carefully to the words emphasized by the radio announcer or TV newscaster. Broadcast commercials are especially sensitive to which words deserve emphasis. *"Big Charlie wants* to sell you a car" is likely to come across better as "Big Charlie wants to sell *you* a car" or better yet, "Big Charlie wants to sell you a *car."* The last of these three focuses your mind on the product while the first one focuses on what Big Charlie wants. Who cares what Big Charlie wants?!

Look over the final version of your talk and determine which words or phrases have the most "punch." Then emphasize these. Typically these are action verbs or clear, concrete nouns: words that clearly describe. Emphasize for *impact.* Now you're *talking!*

Remember that the effectiveness of your delivery will depend on many personal characteristics. Your appearance, manner, and bearing, the use of gestures and body position, eye contact, your voice, and avoiding distracting mannerisms all combine to project a total image. If you have been effective you will come across as being competent, professional, and skillful. Solicit feedback from people you trust about the way you come across. Then have the courage to try on some different behaviors which might improve your speaking image.

The Delivery Critique Form in Figure 10-1 can be useful in getting feedback on your delivery style. Ask someone whose opinions and judgment you trust to complete this form. (Another copy is provided in the Appendix.)

FIGURE 10-1
Delivery critique form

Date: _____

Speaker: _____

Occasion: _____

1. Identify anything distracting in the opening moments of the talk. Check appearance, bearing, image projected, posture, positioning, and so forth.

2. How was the eye contact? Enough to create a strong sense of communication? Did the speaker look too much at some listeners and not enough at others?

3. How effective were the speaker's gestures, facial expressions, movement, and so forth? Identify anything distracting. Cite examples of good gestures.

4. Identify any mispronounced words or unclearly expressed terms.

5. How was the voice? Was the volume appropriate to the occasion? Was there sufficient variation in pitch, rate, timing, to hold listener interest? Was emphasis appropriate and helpful to understanding?

6. Identify any verbalized pauses or nonfluencies. (If this is a problem for the speaker, count the actual number of "um," "uh," "ah," "you know," expressed.)

PROCEDURAL ISSUES IN DELIVERY

Two procedural questions need to be dealt with by any speaker. They are: (1) what kinds of memory devices should be used in delivering the talk?, and (2) to what extent should participation from listeners be permitted or encouraged? Let us consider these two issues briefly.

Memory Devices: Notes-vs-Manuscript. A formal manuscript is seldom appropriate in business presentations. The only advantages of manuscript speaking is that it allows for precise expression and a written record of what exactly was said. This can be important in diplomacy and some formal negotiations. The drawback, of course, is that the speaker *sounds* as though he or she is reading a manuscript rather than communicating sensitively and spontaneously with the audience.

It is almost always more appropriate to extemporize, that is, speak from notes. The complexity and completeness of the notes will vary with individual needs. In almost every case, extemporaneous speaking permits more flexibility and a better sense of communication with your listeners. Senator Everett M. Dirksen enjoyed this speaking flexibility: "I always extemporize. I love the diversions, the detours. Without notes you may digress . . . you may dart . . . and after you have taken on an interrupter, you don't have to flounder around with a piece of paper to find out where in the hell you were."

How much should you put into your notes? Again, this will vary with the individual. I'd suggest putting the attention getter/introduction, the key ideas, the major support information, the summaries, and your conclusion in your notes, to use as a speaking outline. Many speakers prefer using note cards, such as 3" by 5" cards, since they are heavier and make less noise when turned than does a sheet of paper. Also, since the cards are small, you can put only a single idea on each card. This way you are not tempted to read from it as from a larger piece of paper.

Another interesting idea comes from a New York company that teaches presentational speaking to executives. They suggest using *pictures* rather than words on cards to jog the memory.[2] The pictures work, they say, because the brain can translate pictures faster than it can read and assimilate words. Also since there are no words to read, the speaker has to reply on his own language. The result is a more natural, conversational sounding presentation.

The approach is similar to preparing a written outline except you use pictures to convey key ideas. For example, they suggest one "ideagraph" for the subject, one to show the importance of the subject to the audience, four or five for key idea illustrations, one to summarize, and one for conclusions and/or recommendations. The pictures don't have to be recognizable to anyone but the speaker since he or she is the only one to see them.

Another approach is to use pictures for notes but to make those pictures large enough so that they double as visual aids for your audience. As I mentioned in Chapter 9, visual aids can be especially useful in helping the speaker stay on track, as well as in assisting the audience in understanding the message.

The effective speaker will work to minimize the number of notes needed for effective delivery. The fewer words you have written down, the less temptation to read from your note cards and thus inhibit eye contact with your listeners.

One final point. Regardless of whether you use notes, a manuscript, or visual aids it's crucial that you practice the presentation *out loud* before actually delivering it. There is no substitute for this. If you are embarrassed to practice before family or friends, find a quiet spot, preferably some place with a mirror, to practice. Taping your talk in advance, also provides very useful feedback. This practice step is very important because it allows you to hear how you sound as well as whether there are any words or phrases that will be difficult to handle before an audience. When you listen to your taped practice session, be critical. It's better to catch potential weak spots in the presentation here than to have the "real thing" fizzle.

Generating participative responses. The second procedural issue is, to what extent should you seek participation from your listeners. As you've no doubt gathered from earlier chapters, I am a strong believer in audience interactions since I believe such participation leads to the creation of understanding.

The simplest form of such interaction is the question-answer session. This can take several forms. In smaller groups it may be useful to encourage listeners to ask questions *as you present your talk.* For some topics and audiences you may prefer that listeners hold their questions until *after* you've presented

The fewer notes you have written, the less you will be tempted to read to your listeners.

your talk. In some cases you may want to *ask* questions to check for understanding and gain commitment as you go.

The tone you set in handling the first few questions will have an impact on future question-answer interaction. Here are a few tips on how to maximize this give and take.

1.   Avoid embarrassing anyone by putting them on the spot with one of your questions.

2.   Avoid expressing negative evaluations of questions received—verbally or *nonverbally*. Any question asked should be regarded as a request for more information. Such requests show listener interest in gaining understanding of what you have to say. That's the same goal you have! Accept the old dictum that "The only stupid question is the one you don't ask." Never put down someone's question as stupid or irrelevant.

3.   Restate the question for the rest of your audience before answering it—especially when all listeners may not have heard it originally.

4.   When a listener makes a statement, react to it (even if it doesn't require an answer). Don't just let a remark hang there in dead air. Say something to indicate agreement, disagreement, or, at least, appreciation for sharing the thought. A simple "thanks for sharing that idea with us, Sue" or "good point, Chris" can go a long way toward encouraging additional participation.

5.   Don't let a single questioner dominate. Encourage everyone who has questions or comments to speak up. If you have one person who is persistent in overparticipating you may suggest that you'll get together with them after the presentation to clarify things.

6.   In some cases you may want to "plant" one or two questions to ensure that the question session will get off the ground. Prearrange to have a few important questions asked—preferably questions which will stimulate further comments from others.

7.   Don't let the questions get too far afield of your topic. If they do, you may wind up spending too much time on irrelevant issues.

8.   Answer questions directly and candidly. If you don't know an answer, say so. Don't try to bluff. If it's an important enough question, offer to find out and get back to the questioner.

9.   Be patient. Some of your listeners won't grasp the message as quickly as you think they should. Keep trying to help them.

One final thought. When you feel you have presented your talk as effectively as possible and you have handled a reasonable number of questions—quit. Don't drag it out. As an anonymous wag once said, "No speech can be entirely bad if it is short." Taking excessive time can damage your presentation.

Overcoming apprehension (one more time). Back in Chapter 4 I talked about reducing the anxiety you are likely to feel in many presentation situations. If you still feel uncomfortable about giving your talk, here is one last suggestion: To overcome your fear, ask yourself what is the worst thing that could happen when you make your presentation. Then plan how to deal with it, if it *does* happen. For example, maybe your fear is that you'll lose your train of thought while speaking. The worst thing that could happen in that case is that you will stop speaking and just stand there. How will you deal with that? Probably the best thing to do is to say "excuse me" to your audience while you look at your notes to recall what you wanted to say next. Once you've collected your thoughts, proceed with the presentation. Now that's not so horrible, is it? In other words, admit your worst fears and conquer them in your own mind. Then you can put them out of your head because you have planned what you'll do if they happen while you're speaking. (Be careful not to dwell on possible goofs—just acknowledge the *remote* possibility that they *could* happen.)

Remember, your audience wants you to succeed and you *will* if you are *prepared*. Know your material, look your best, take a second to organize your notes, and finally *begin speaking*.

"Well, I see my time is up . . ."

When you've finished talking, quit!

Reprinted from the *Saturday Evening Post*, July 25, 1959. Used by permission of Joe Zeis.

DELIVERING THE PRESENTATION

Chapter 10. A summary of key ideas

1. Our personal characteristics project a total image as we speak to others. Much of this image comes across nonverbally.
2. The business speaker should be sensitive to at least six classes of nonverbal communication:
   (a) norms of personal space and communication distances
   (b) personal appearance
   (c) body movements, posture, and gestures
   (d) touching behavior
   (e) facial expression and eye contact
   (f) vocal cues and paralanguage
3. Violating norms of personal space can create discomfort for listeners. Positioning ourselves too close to their personal "bubble" may cause discomfort; too far away conveys aloofness.
4. Personal appearance should be *appropriate* to the speaking situation. Avoid the hairdo or clothing which may distract the listener from the message.
5. Gestures and body movements convey dynamism. They also serve to emphasize and provide nonverbal transitions indicating the flow of your message for the listener.
6. Touching behaviors can break through psychological barriers between people but may be inappropriate or impossible in presentation situations.
7. Facial expression and eye contact may be the most important nonverbal variable. People expect eye contact when communicating with others.
8. The voice communicates nonverbally as well as verbally. Key aspects of voice and paralanguage are:
   (a) pronunciation
   (b) voice quality
   (c) verbalized pauses or nonfluencies
   (d) emphasis
9. Except for the rare case where a written record of a talk is needed, extemporaneous delivery using only notes should be used.
10. There is no substitute for *practicing* a talk out loud.
11. Audience participation, question-answer sessions being the most common form, leads to the creation of better understanding. The speaker often sets the tone and climate for such give and take.

NOTES

1. Mark L. Knapp. *Nonverbal Communication in Human Interaction,* 2nd ed. (New York: Holt, Rinehart and Winston, 1978), p. 243.
2. As described in "A $900 Lesson in Podim Power," *Fortune,* August 1977, p. 196.

A COMMENT ABOUT THE FINAL TWO CHAPTERS

In chapters Eleven and Twelve I'm going to shift gears a bit. I want to go behind the scenes and look at some more theoretical considerations as they apply to persuasive and informative speaking. Being theoretical does not preclude being practical. Indeed, good theory is good because it *is* practical. I'll continue to suggest specific applications and suggestions which you can immediately apply.

Chapter Eleven deals with persuasion. In a legitimate sense, all communication attempts to be persuasive; we always have *some* impact on our hearers (although it may be quite different than we intended!) which will cause them to be changed or to be influenced. This is persuasion. Because persuasion is so omnipresent, this chapter is longer than Chapter Twelve which addresses the informative or instructional talk. The distinction between the two forms of discourse is very hazy.

Instructional communication is a special class of persuasive communication. For that reason, I've prepared a separate shorter chapter to look at some of its special characteristics.

An understanding of such communication theory is, I feel, indispensable to the business communicator.

11

PERSUASIVE MESSAGES:
how they work (when they do)

OBJECTIVES OF CHAPTER 11

After studying this chapter, the reader should be able to

1. Define and give examples of persuasive communication situations relevant to his or her occupation.
2. Explain the value of learning about communication theory.
3. Describe the parts of the persuasive model presented in the chapter and show how each can affect communications success.
4. Identify four characteristics of attitudes and explain how these affect personality and behavior.
5. Define and describe the concept of personal *values*.
6. Name and describe the theory behind the two approaches to attitude and behavior change described in the chapter.
7. Name the four alternatives available to a person who is faced with psychological imbalance between his or her attitude/value system and some new information received.
8. Describe the two types of reinforcement used to strengthen behaviors under the conditioning approach.
9. Describe five or six generalizations about persuasion (as supported by research) in each of the following areas:
   (a) source (speaker) variables
   (b) message characteristics
   (c) receiver (listener) variables
   (d) group influences on listeners

In the simplest sense, persuasive presentations are those that try to get your listeners to do or think something they wouldn't do or think without your encouragement. More specifically, persuasion can be defined as a conscious effort to modify or change the attitudes, beliefs, or behavior of other people through the use of communication. Communication, of course, has been described throughout this book as the creation of mutual understanding and common meanings.

Since persuasive communication aims at changing attitudes and behaviors, it is useful to understand where these attitudes and behaviors come from, and how we can motivate people to change them. Although this book has not been heavily theoretical (as promised), we can learn a lot by studying some underlying reasoning behind the process of persuasion. Such study is based in *theory*. As communication scholar William Haney has said, "If we are to communicate with others, serve as subordinate, manage others, and the like, we must have *some kind of theory*—valid or not, conscious or not—about human motivation and relationships. Otherwise we will be unable to function at all. If we are to control or to influence behavior—our own at any rate—we must be capable of predicting reasonably accurately the response of others—and of ourselves."[1]

A theory is a way of explaining things. It can serve a unifying function by pulling together descriptive and explanatory statements about matters that we're interested in. And perhaps most important for our discussion here, *theory helps us make more accurate predictions* about how people will respond to given situations. The social sciences have provided some excellent theories about persuasion, several of which we will look at later in the chapter.

This chapter will be broken down into three general areas. First, we will consider an overview of what goes into persuasive communication. Understanding the variables involved gives us some ideas of what "strings" we have to pull; what factors we have to work with to improve our persuasive abilities. The second general section of this chapter will look at several theories of attitude change with an eye towards improving our predictive abilities. Finally, the third section of the chapter will present a list of propositions derived from the vast quantity of research in persuasive communication. These propositions should provide the business speaker with specific ideas of what to seek and what to avoid as we try to persuade other people.

AN OVERVIEW MODEL OF PERSUASIVE COMMUNICATION

The purpose of a model like the one presented in Figure 11-1 is to identify the variables and indicate something about the process of persuasive communication. Take a moment to look at the model before we discuss it further. Let's consider the parts of this model.

Scope and cost of the persuasive objective. As the figure indicates, a primary variable which affects the whole situation is the scope and cost of the persuasive objective. *Scope* refers to how difficult it is for the listener to comply with the message's persuasive request. *Cost* refers to how much tradeoff the listener must make to comply. Both scope and cost can be psychological in nature or can refer to physical/tangible resistances to change. For example, getting your boss to grant a 20 percent budget increase may be difficult because (1) the company has been losing money and literally cannot afford to give you more (physical/tangible resistance), and (2) your boss has "gone on the record" (i.e., made public statements) against any budget increases without a compensating improvement in company earnings. When people are asked to change their behavior in some way that causes them to lose face, the

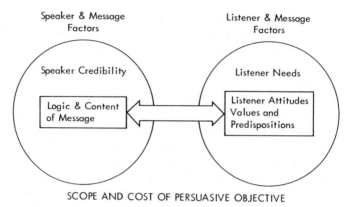

FIGURE 11-1
A persuasive model

psychological cost can be high. When the persuasive objective is a grandiose program such as a major reorganization, the scope will be broad. The wider the scope and the higher the cost, the more difficult your communication situation is.

Try to empathize with your listeners to identify scope and costs from *their point of view.* Accurate prediction here will help you to anticipate the degree of persuasive effort you'll need to expend to get the desired result.

Speaker and message factors. The left half of the model represents speaker and message factors. These include credibility (which we discussed briefly in Chapter Five) as well as the logic and content of the message.

None of these factors is likely to remain constant throughout a persuasive effort. For example, your speaker credibility can change as you speak. Because you're such a handsome devil, your credibility may be quite positive as you get up to start speaking, based perhaps on your personal appearance. It may then drop a bit as your opening remarks are viewed as hesitant or uninteresting. It may rise sharply as you present a perceptive analysis of a problem and then fall off again as you offer a solution to that problem which is regarded as undesirable by your listeners. When you finish speaking, and handle a question and answer session, your credibility may again rise. The point is that speaker credibility is not a constant. It varies from time to time.

Similarly, the logic and content of your message will fluctuate in its persuasiveness. No one can be an absolute spellbinder *all* the time. Try to recognize the strongest points in your persuasive appeal. Then arrange these in such a way as to convince your listeners. (Chapter Six talked about patterns of arrangement.)

Listener and message factors. Factors affecting your listeners' responses also fluctuate. We are all motivated by personal needs. But these needs vary widely among people and within the same person over time. We constantly change our priorities. This is clearly supported by psychological theory.

The classic work by psychologist Abraham Maslow in the 1940s concluded that our needs have differing strength at different times. Indeed, Maslow concluded that needs can be arranged in a heirarchy ranging from our basic physiological needs (food, water, avoidance of temperature extremes, and so forth), on up through security, social, esteem, and self actualization (a sense of accomplishment) needs. As one of these needs becomes satisfied (at least temporarily), other higher order needs provide the motivation for action. A simple example of this in a speaking situation might be as follows. You have been asked to convince a group of listeners of the importance of improving the quality of workmanship in their products. Although your appeals to their sense of worker pride (self-actualization) may work for some of your listeners, we cannot assume it'll work for all. For some, there may be unsatisfied lower level needs which would have stronger appeal. For example, perhaps the need to be accepted among one's fellow workers (social needs) dictates that that worker *not* produce unusually high quality products lest she make the other employees look bad by comparison. The persuader appealing to self-actualization would not succeed here unless the social need issue is addressed too. Your listener's needs are highly variable.

Some characteristics of attitudes. The objective of most persuasive communication is to change or modify attitudes and behavior in some way. In its simplest sense, an attitude is a way we have come to think about some particular thing or class of things; it is a *habit of thought*. These thought patterns often dictate our behavior. To be classified as an attitude, several characteristics must be present.

First, *attitudes have some sort of object in mind.* To say that "Tom has a positive attitude," is an incomplete statement. More realistically, we would have to say "Tom has a positive attitude *toward the opportunities for advancement in this company."* This statement provides an attitude object. We can learn considerably more about Tom by having his attitude object attached to the above statement than we could otherwise.

Second, *attitudes have direction, degree, and intensity.* Attitudes are characterized by an orientation toward objects. And these orientations can vary in degree and intensity. The *direction* of an attitude indicates such things as positive or negative viewpoints; liking or disliking. The *degree* or *intensity* indicates how much the person may like or dislike a particular thing; the level of conviction with which the attitude is held.

A third characteristic is that *attitudes are learned.* We develop attitudes through our direct or indirect experience with an object or person. Our direct experiences are perhaps the most important contributors to attitude formation. However, the effects of indirect experiences on attitude development should not be minimized. For example, we may have had direct experience with an automobile salesman which was unpleasant and caused us to have negative attitudes toward that person, and perhaps the whole process of buying a car. Indirect experiences, such as other people's "horror stories" about car salesmen, can serve to reinforce that negative attitude.

A fourth and final characteristic is that attitudes are *relatively stable and enduring*. Attitudes normally do not change quickly. Neither, however, are they absolute, rigid, or permanent. (If they were, persuasion attempts would be futile.) Depending on the individual, attitudes tend to resist change for several reasons.

Among these reasons, there is *personal ownership* of the attitude. We hold a particular attitude because it "feels good" mentally. It also tends to fit together with our other attitudes and values. Any change logically requires readjustment of other habits of thought which becomes a fairly complicated process. We find ourselves rethinking whole sets of assumptions which had served us well in the past. This can be pretty uncomfortable. This discomfort provides the motivation for accepting persuasive appeals as we'll see in a moment.

A second reason that attitudes tend to be fairly stable is that we sometimes state them publicly. When we have vocalized an attitude, there becomes an increasing motivation to stick with that attitude. To back down from it may indicate a sign of weakness, a loss of face.

A third type of resistance to changes arises when our attitudes are solidified by our affiliations with others. We tend to socialize with others who have attitudes similar to our own. This is simply more comfortable than being with people who hold radically different ideas. Few people will go out of their way to solicit information that is likely to disrupt the attitudes they hold. Consider from your own experience how often you read or listen to messages from a political leader, for example, whom you disagree with.

The concept of values. One other listener factor pointed up by our simple model is the value system of the message receiver. Values are closely related to attitudes but tend to be even more enduring. A value is our concept of the desirable. It is our personal expression of the worth of something. For example, honesty is a highly regarded personal value for most people. Beauty or agility or having white teeth may be values of varying importance to different people.

Like attitudes, values tend to fit together into patterns for people. We develop our own value *system* which evolves over time. As we grow older our values—our perceptions of the desirable—change. The teenager's dream of a "hot car" gives way to the economical stationwagon; the importance of career success gives way to a satisfying retirement. As we make the passage through life, our value structures adjust.

Assuming that others share the same values as you can lead to miscommunication.

In addition to ageing, changes in our day-to-day roles can affect values. The newly appointed supervisor may suddenly value employee reliability much more than he did as a rank and file worker. The birth of a child often finds the new parents or grandparents reassessing their values. A person's values and attitudes serve as guides in choosing what one perceives and how one behaves in fulfilling life's many roles.

The effective persuader recognizes these factors, and develops sensitivity to cues which indicate the strength and stability of attitudes and values. From these insights the message is tailored for maximum impact.

One final thought about changing attitudes. The more persistent an individual's experience with an attitude object, the less likely it would be that his or her attitude may be changed by a single message presentation.[2] Don't rule out the possibility of using multiple media and exposures to expose your persuasive request. This is *often* necessary.

The ever changing nature of speaker variables as well as listener need variables, makes persuasion quite tricky. The speaker should be aware before he or she goes into a persuasive talk of how difficult the achievement of a persuasive objective can be. Figure 11-2 illustrates the relative difficulty of

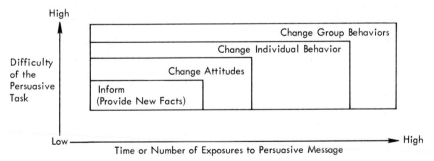

FIGURE 11-2
The relative difficulty of persuasion

persuasive tasks. As we can see, bringing new information to people (which in a sense is a very mild form of persuasion) is relatively easy, and requires relatively little time or few exposures to the persuasive message. However, as we attempt to change attitudes or values, individual behaviors, and group behavior, our task difficulty is magnified.

ATTITUDE AND BEHAVIOR CHANGES: TWO APPROACHES

There are two general approaches to changing others (including getting them to do what you want). The first is to give them some new information which, in turn, causes them to change their attitudes and, hopefully, their behavior. (One common form of behavior change sought in persuasive speaking is from doing nothing to doing something.) This, of course, is based in the assumption that people *do* things that are consistent with their attitudes. The second approach seeks to change the behavior *first,* assuming that the attitudes will change later. Some persuaders, and more often, some instructors, get listeners to try on a new behavior—have a "hands-on" experience—even though it runs counter to their normal activities. After the new behavior is tried, the persuader reinforces (rewards) the listener causing him or her to continue the new behavior. Attitude change comes about as the new behavior begins to feel comfortable.

Figure 11-3 shows the direction of persuasive effort for each approach. The first approach described above makes use of a *consistency principle* or a

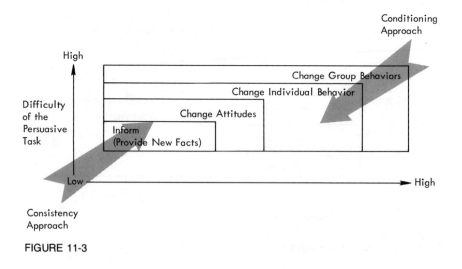

FIGURE 11-3

balance theory. The second approach is based in *conditioning* theories. Of these two, the consistency principle is the most frequently used in persuasive communication and is most soundly supported by research. But conditioning can have interesting effects too. Let's look a bit closer at these two approaches.

THE CONSISTENCY PRINCIPLE

In Chapter Six, I discussed a simple four-step model for persuasive communication. The four steps included gaining attention, establishing a need, solving that need, and providing an action step for the listener. That model, which is repeated in Figure 11-4, applies the consistency principle.

Since the early 1940s, psychologists have developed a number of consistency theories which apply nicely to communication. Each of these theories is based on three premises.

1. People prefer a state of psychological equilibrium (that is, harmony, consistency, balance, or freedom from anxiety).
2. Loss of a sense of equilibrium creates a feeling of tension or drive.
3. The result of the tension or drive is an attempt to restore the state of equilibrium.

Premise number one is pretty much self-evident. People prefer to have their thoughts all fit into neat and reasonable patterns. People like to avoid anxiety-producing conflicts in the ways they think. We like to have the world make sense.

Premise number two, a loss of equilibrium, needs a little more explanation. As discussed in Chapter Six, where I first presented the persuasive model, it is important to create a need, dilemma, or problem situation in the mind of

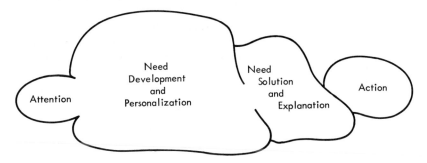

FIGURE 11-4
A problem-solution persuasive model

your message receiver. If that is done effectively, this need provides the loss of psychological equilibrium for your listener. This sort of imbalance is not an unusual occurrence. We all experience disequilibrium even in unintentional, everyday situations. Say, for example, one of your friendliest employees suddenly shouts angrily at you. Or a dealer who has always given you excellent service on your automobile suddenly appears uncaring and turns in shoddy work. Or a community leader, whom you have looked up to, is suddenly arrested for a sex crime. These kinds of things can be very disturbing. They create a disharmony between your established attitudes, in these cases toward particular people, and the new information you have received.

If that disharmony impinges upon your psychological or physical needs, it is likely to be especially disturbing. If the conflicting information presents no threat to your needs or your ways of thinking, little if any dissonance will result. In other words, the greater the threat to your world of understanding, the greater the dissonance or anxiety; the less the threat, the less the dissonance. The task of the persuader is to intentionally create this psychological imbalance as part of the persuasive process.

Premise number three: restoring equilibrium. Once dissonance is experienced, we have several options available to deal with it. These include the following:

1. *Simply ignore the dissonance.* Different people have differing thresholds at which dissonance bothers them. Some are very sensitive and must take dissonance reducing measures immediately. Others can cope with a great deal of such psychological imbalance without serious discomfort.
2. *Reject the conflicting new information.* The tendency to reject conflicting ideas has been described by Jesse Nirenberg, an industrial psychologist, in this manner:

> As people move through life they build up a wardrobe of ideas and points of view. These ideas are comfortable. They fit well. They suit the taste of the individual and he feels at ease with them. Like an old shoe, they have become shaped to his contours.
>
> He's reluctant to discard any of these ideas for something new. When he tries on new ideas they feel awkward. They're not cut quite right for him. He misses the security of the old ideas, and sometimes scarcely recognizes himself when holding the new ones . . .
>
> The truth is that he isn't likely to be swayed merely by logic to give up any of his ideas for new ones.[3]

3. *Depreciate or devalue the conflicting information.* Here the respondent essentially attacks the credibility of the new information. If the new information says, for example, that the manager's trusted secretary is being rude to other employees, he might rationalize it by saying "So what? I believe in being

assertive even if you step on a few toes. People respect you for it. Besides, my secretary only reacts in that way under extreme and infrequent situations." When one chooses this means of coping with dissonance, he or she will usually get busy producing evidence that the conflicting information is, in fact, wrong.

4. *Reject the old attitude and accept the new.* Although this is generally the most difficult means of reducing dissonance for most people, it does occur from time to time. If it didn't, persuasive attempts would be futile. Since attitudes are learned by direct and indirect experience, they can be unlearned. When new information which runs counter to the existing attitude is offered, some people will accept the new information. People do change.

How do you use the consistency principle in persuasion? As persuaders, we intentionally create dissonance in the minds of our listeners. We intentionally throw them "out of balance." Once this has occurred, the options cited become available to our listeners. If our need development is communicated clearly enough and is personalized so that they really feel it, they are not likely to choose option one, ignoring the problem. If our credibility is sufficiently high and our message appropriately developed for clarity, they won't select options two or three, rejecting or devaluing the new information. That leaves option four—attitude change. The result—successful persuasion.

THE CONDITIONING PRINCIPLE

Looking back to our diagram in Figure 11-3, we see another approach which aims at changing behavior *first*. Attitude changes become secondary. There are many variations of this approach but all are based in behavioral psychology as developed by B. F. Skinner. The objective is to (1) get people to try on some new behavior and (2) reinforce the new behavior with some reward.

At the heart of any such change efforts is the premise that future behavior is influenced by the outcomes of past behavior. If the outcome immediately following an act was in some way rewarding, we are likely to do the behavior again. If the response was punishing, we're likely to not do it again, unless we prefer punishment to other available outcomes. Some people do.

Communicators can provide three types of responses to behaviors: positive reinforcement, negative reinforcement, or no observable response at all. The effects of each of these upon the behavior are shown on page 180.

As communicators, our reinforcement is frequently verbal (as opposed to giving tangible rewards). There are some questions about just how far we can go with verbal approval or disapproval as a motivator of change. Theoretically, it should work indefinitely so long as appropriate "schedules of reinforcement"

BEHAVIOR RESPONSES TO DIFFERENT REINFORCEMENT

Types of Responses to Employee Behavior	Effective on the Recurrence of the Behavior
positive reinforcement	tends to increase or strengthen the recurrence of such behavior
negative reinforcement	tends to decrease or weaken the recurrence of such behavior *unless* the receiver is seeking negative reinforcement to coincide with his or her self-image
no reinforcement (ignore the behavior)	tends to decrease or weaken the recurrence of such behavior. Can lead to extinction of the behavior.

are used. There are two main reinforcement schedules: *continuous* and *intermittent*.

Continuous reinforcement means that the individual receives reinforcement (a compliment or supportive statement) every time he or she does the desired behavior. This approach is useful when the person is being taught a new activity and needs to be shored up to develop confidence in this new ability. People learn very quickly, at least initially, under continuous reinforcement. You can readily observe this when teaching a child how to do something like, say, catching a ball. Each time the ball is caught you praise the child and the child will develop this skill very quickly. The principle also generally holds for employees working on unfamiliar tasks.

There are three main problems with continuous reinforcement. First, it takes too much time—and therefore costs a great deal—in communication effort. It is just not feasible always to compliment each action done right—especially when you are working with a group of listeners. Secondly, there is a problem of "inflation." Just as dollars lose value when too many are in circulation, verbal approval statements are cheapened by overuse. The third problem is that once continuous reinforcement is expected, it is tough to wean people away from it without certain risks. If we suddenly drop continuous reinforcement—that is, we no longer express verbal approval for each good behavior—the message to our worker may be that the behavior is no longer appropriate and should be stopped. In short we may extinguish the desired behavior.

The drawbacks to continuous reinforcement are largely overcome by using intermittent reinforcement. Here we do not express approval of every action but instead use another system to allocate compliments. We may decide to express approval at some interval such as each time a whole series of actions—say a new sales approach—is successfully used.

The best approach seems to be to use continuous reinforcement when new behaviors are being developed and then gradually move to an intermittent schedule so that the desired performance won't be inadvertently extinguished. In other words, shift the listeners' expectations so that longer intervals between reinforcement are seen as normal.

Finally, we need to be aware that the use of praise coupled with appropriate criticism doesn't always produce desired results. When you're dealing with human communication and motivation, nothing is a sure thing.

Once new behaviors have been tried and found desirable, attitudes change too. Let me give an example of the use of the conditioning approach in a persuasive presentation. Suppose that there has been a general resistance to the use of some special features of your company's new computerized telephone system. Your objective is to persuade your listeners to maximize their productivity by using the system's special capabilities.

A conditioning approach might get them to try the different features on specially rigged demonstration phones, reinforcing them each time they get it right. The attitudes toward the system are likely to soften as your listeners get familiar with and begin to use the equipment.

Obviously from this example, a conditioning approach has important applications for instructional presentations as well as persuasive talks. Also obvious is the crucial role played by listener involvement and participation—a theme I've been hammering on for eleven chapters now.

Whether you choose to apply the conditioning approach or the consistency principle, awareness of some theory will help you be a better persuader. Take the opportunity to read more about these and other social science theories. Then apply them as you communicate.

SOME GENERALIZATIONS DERIVED FROM RESEARCH IN PERSUASION

The remainder of this chapter summarizes some key findings of persuasion research. I've attempted to express these concisely; they are, therefore, somewhat incomplete. If additional detail is needed or if you are interested in how this research was conducted, more information can be found in persuasion theory textbooks or professional journals in communication. I've listed several sources on the notes page at the end of this chapter.

These generalizations about persuasion will be discussed under four categories. Generalizations relating to

1. the *source* of a persuasive message (the speaker)
2. *message* variables

3.   variables affecting the *receiver* of the persuasive message
4.   *group pressure* and influences on persuasion.

GENERALIZATIONS ABOUT THE SOURCE
OF A PERSUASIVE MESSAGE

1.   Attitude or behavior change in the advocated direction is more likely to occur when the sender of a message is perceived as highly credible. Credibility is made up of your listener's perceptions of trustworthiness, competence, dynamism, and objectivity. The speaker who is viewed as being honest, having expertise with regard to the topic under discussion, being enthusiastic or animated, and having no hidden motivations (secret goals in mind) will be regarded as high in credibility. Experiments have shown that even a speech that is nonsense (sentences logically unrelated to one another) is treated as if it were important when the speaker carries high prestige.

2.   When a speaker arouses anger or resentment, the receivers' attitudes will be unfavorable toward the person. Listeners will also tend to have a negative impression of groups, goals, or enterprises with which that speaker is identified. Conversely, when a speaker is viewed very favorably, he or she reflects a positive image of the organization, goals, groups, and so forth.

3.   When the speaker is unknown to his listeners, he or she can raise credibility by (a) describing relevant or novel personal experiences, (b) decreasing the number of non-fluencies in the presentation (i.e., verbalized pauses: "hemming and hawing"), (c) being well-organized, and (d) using correct pronounciation and effective delivery.

4.   The credibility of a speaker can be enhanced by a favorable introduction, so long as the introducer carries high credibility. In other words, a "halo effect" can be bestowed upon a speaker by someone who introduces him or her.

5.   Listeners tend to be favorable towards messages from speakers whom they regard as being similar to themselves. If a speaker can convince his audience that they and he are the same in essence, the audience is more likely to concur with his ideas.

6.   The persuasiveness of any message, even one attributed to a respected speaker, disappears over time. The impact of the highly credible speaker can be reinstated by reminding the listeners of what he or she said.

7.   If an audience regards a speaker unfavorably, the speaker can still be effective if his identification is delayed until after the message is delivered or the audience perceives him as arguing against his own self-interest.

8.   The greater the perceived differences between speaker and listeners, the greater the likelihood of barriers to communication arising.

9.   The speaker's ability to empathize accurately with the audience is a key to effective persuasion and communication. One who is insensitive to his or her listeners' needs is unlikely to succeed.

GENERALIZATIONS ABOUT THE NATURE OF THE PERSUASIVE MESSAGE ITSELF

1.   People need to be prepared for messages, especially those likely to evoke emotional responses. Giving the listeners the proper "preparatory set" greatly increases their recognition and attention level.

2.   If a message initially arouses exceptionally *intense* feelings of anxiety, people tend to ignore the further content of that message. Listeners will tune out.

3.   There is a tendency for listeners to protect themselves from disturbing experiences such as arguments against their prevailing attitudes or beliefs. This conflict-avoiding behavior results in the listener paying little attention to opposing arguments. Listeners will tune out the speaker if they suspect his message will not confirm their beliefs and opinions.

4.   A one-sided presentation is more effective than a two-sided presentation if (a) the listener already agrees with the speaker, or (b) the listener is not later exposed to counter arguments for which he has no answers.

5.   A two-sided presentation is more effective than a one-sided if (a) the listener initially disagrees with the sender, or (b) the listener may later be exposed to counter arguments.

6.   The persuasive message can provide an individual with defenses against attacks on his beliefs. This principle called *"innoculation"* is similar to medical innoculations. The listener is provided with a small dose of the counter-arguments, just as a person may be subject to a mild dose of a disease. Responses to those counter-arguments are provided in the message, thus permitting the listener to fight off counter-arguments in the future.

7.   If the listener is likely to have relatively low interest in the message, the major argument should be presented first. A direct order of presentation, "big idea first," is both efficient and persuasive in such cases. If the listener has high interest and probable resistance to the speaker's ideas, the "big idea" should be presented only after the reasoning is carefully explained.

8.   Persuasive *logical* arguments tend to be more effective when directed towards audiences of high intelligence. *Emotional* arguments will have greater influence on listeners of lower intelligence.

9.   Messages that appeal to more than one of the senses, that is, use multiple media, influence more effectively than those that appeal to one sense only.

GENERALIZATIONS ABOUT THE RECEIVERS OF PERSUASIVE MESSAGES

1. Message receivers selectively receive and interpret messages in terms of their existing knowledge, attitudes, beliefs, and current needs.
2. A listener is more *receptive* to a message that is consistent with his or her existing knowledge, attitudes, and beliefs than to one that is not.
3. A listener will *retain* messages that are consistent with his or her existing knowledge, attitudes, and beliefs more effectively than ones that are not.
4. Messages phrased in terms of listener interests and needs are more successful than messages oriented to the sender. A "you viewpoint" is imperative for effective persuasion.
5. Features or recommendations should be phrased as benefits to the listener. A feature describes a characteristic of the product, service, or recommendation of the speaker. A benefit can be viewed as a "what this means to you" statement. The effective persuader persistently and explicitly relates features to listener benefits.
6. Message receivers with a high personal esteem are less readily influenced than those with low self-esteem.
7. The overtly hostile listener, or the excessively apathetic or withdrawn listener, is not likely to be influenced by persuasive messages.
8. Mental or verbal participation by a message receiver improves the chance that that listener will be persuaded.

GENERALIZATIONS ABOUT THE EFFECTS OF GROUP INFLUENCE ON PERSUASIVE MESSAGES

1. A listener is influenced by the frame of reference which he believes those around him share. The tendency to conform with opinions of that group are directly related to the individual's motivation to maintain membership in the group. Such peer pressure will influence the degree to which a listener accepts the speaker's call for action.
2. If the speaker's message runs counter to the norms of the group, a listener's tendency to accept that message is inversely proportional to the value he places on group membership. If he has a relatively low regard for his group membership, he is likely to accept the message; if a high regard for group membership, he will reject the persuasive message.
3. Members of an audience will look to other listeners within that audience to confirm or refute arguments. People look for primarily nonverbal cues to determine the accuracy, or acceptability of a persuader's message.

4. If the persuader attempts to bring about changes in an individual which requires deviation from the norms of his or her group, they are very likely to be resisted and consequently unsuccessful.

A final note. These generalizations about persuasive communication are just that—generalizations. They are, however, supported by empirical research which seeks to measure such things. And they should provide the business communicator with some things to think about.

PERSUASIVE MESSAGES: HOW THEY WORK WHEN THEY DO

Chapter 11. A summary of key ideas

1. Persuasion is getting listeners to do or think something they otherwise wouldn't. It involves modifying attitudes, beliefs, and behavior through communication.
2. We all base our actions on some kind of theory—implicit or expressed—which helps us explain and predict. Good theory improves our understanding and our ability to predict outcomes accurately.
3. Models of communication help us see interrelationships and identify variables that affect communication. In persuasion these variables include
    (a) the scope and cost of the persuasive objective as perceived by the persuadee
    (b) speaker and message characteristics
    (c) listener characteristics.
4. Persuasive communication aims to modify attitudes (that is, change or strengthen them). To do so we should understand some of the characteristics of attitudes.
5. Attitudes are habits of thought which
    (a) have some object in mind
    (b) have direction, degree, and intensity
    (c) are learned through direct and indirect experience
    (d) are relatively stable and enduring.
6. Values are an individual's concept of the desirable. Like attitudes, values fit together into systems of belief. Values can be shifted but rather reluctantly. Differences in assumptions about others' values result in communication breakdowns.

7. Two theoretical approaches to attitude and behavior change are the consistency principle and the conditioning principle. The former seeks to change attitudes by causing psychological discomfort which can be alleviated by the persuadee accepting the persuader's recommendations. The latter seeks to have the persuadee try on new behavior with the belief that attitude change will follow as those new behaviors are reinforced.

8. Persuasion research supports some generalizations about variables affecting speaker characteristics, message factors, receiver characteristics, and group pressures on listeners. A series of generalizations about each were presented.

NOTES

1. William V. Haney, *Communication and Interpersonal Relations,* 4th ed. (Homewood, IL: Richard D. Irwin, Inc., 1979), p. 193.
2. Ronald L. Applbaum and Karl W.E. Anatol, *Strategies for Persuasive Communication* (Columbus, OH: Charles E. Merrill, 1974), p. 22.
3. Jesse S. Nirenberg, *Getting Through to People* (Englewood Cliffs, NJ: Prentice-Hall, 1963), p. 114.

The following is a list of sources of additional information about persuasion theory:

ANDERSEN, KENNETH E. *Persuasion: Theory and Practice* (Boston: Allyn and Bacon, 1978).

APPLBAUM, RONALD L. AND KARL W.E. ANATOL. *Strategies for Persuasive Communication* (Columbus, OH: Charles E. Merrill, 1974).

BEISECKER, THOMAS D. AND DONN W. PARSON (Eds.). *The Process of Social Influence* (Englewood Cliffs, NJ: Prentice-Hall, 1972).

BETTINGHAUS, ERWIN P. *Persuasive Communication,* 2nd ed., (New York: Holt, Rhinehart and Winston, 1973).

BREMBECK, WINSTON L. *Persuasion: A Means of Social Influence,* 2nd ed. (Englewood Cliffs, NJ: Prentice-Hall, 1976).

CRONKHEIT, GARY. *Persuasion: Speech and Behavioral Change* (Indianapolis: Bobbs-Merrill, 1969).

KARLINS, MARVIN AND HERBERT I. ABELSON. *Persuasion: How Opinions and Attitudes Are Changed,* 2nd ed., (New York: Springer Publishing Co., 1970).

LARSON, CHARLES U. *Persuasion: Reception and Responsibility* (Belmont, CA: Wadsworth Publishing Co., 1973).

LUND, PHILIP R. *Compelling Selling: A Framework for Persuasion* (New York: AMACOM, 1974).

MILLER, GERALD R. AND MICHAEL BURGOON. *New Techniques of Persuasion* (New York: Harper & Row, Pub., 1973).

OLIVER, ROBERT T. *The Psychology of Persuasive Speech* (New York: D. McKay, 1968).

ROSS, RAYMOND S. *Persuasion: Communication and Interpersonal Relations* (Englewood Cliffs, NJ: Prentice-Hall, 1974).

12

INSTRUCTIONAL
PRESENTATIONS:
special considerations

OBJECTIVES FOR CHAPTER 12

After studying this chapter, the reader should be able to

1. Describe five advantages in using measurable learning objectives when giving an instructional talk.
2. Name three reasons some speakers resist the use of measureable objectives.
3. Identify and give examples of the three parts of an effective learning object.
4. Cite five examples of concrete, action-oriented words or phrases which are useful in expressing behavioral objectives.

I had to restrain myself from making this a three-word chapter: USE LEARNING OBJECTIVES. Instead I'll take several pages of lucid text to make an important recommendation to all who have the opportunity to present instructional talks: Use learning objectives.

In business presentations we are concerned with *functional* communication; messages that answer questions, that explain reasoning, that recommend action. In short, presentations that get listeners to *do something*. A crucial part of the persuasive model we discussed earlier, is the *action* step. The difference between such functional communications and other types of messages, say literature, poetry, or story telling, is like the difference between agriculture and culture. Business presentations are more concerned with the yield. (Hold the manure jokes, please.)

So how do we know what your yield is? In persuasion we can usually see if we have succeeded by observing whether or not our listener does what we want. But in instructional, information-giving presentations, we must be content with observing whether or not our listener does what we want. No, that's not a misprint. Our success in informational presentations can be measured as surely as our success in persuasive. IF, we use learning objectives.

Before I go on, let me clarify that the terms "learning objectives," and "behavior objectives" (and any other variation on that theme) mean the same thing so far as this discussion is concerned. I'll use them interchangeably for variety. "Objectives"—that is, clear, measurable goals or targets—is the key word.

ADVANTAGES OF MEASURABLE OBJECTIVES

The notion of target setting and measuring performance against such targets has been reprinted throughout this book. Indeed, in Chapter One, I stressed that this book aims to help readers *change* their *communication behaviors,* not just learn about presentational speaking.

In instructional presentations, behavior objectives tie learning and thought to action. Behavior of some sort is the only observable manifestation of thinking. So to be functional—to accomplish some predetermined communication objective—we must have observable behavior as the goal of our presentation.

There are at least five important advantages in using behavior objectives:

1. Behavior objectives help the speaker keep an *applications focus.* When we keep in mind specific things we'd like our listeners to *do* as a result of our presentation or briefing we help them see the relevance of what we're saying. When relevance is clear, it's much easier to hold attention and establish understanding. A presentation "to help employees understand our retirement benefits" (non-behavior objective) is likely to be less applications-focused than "to teach each employee to calculate his or her own retirement benefits earned to date" (behavior objective). I strongly suspect the second would be more focused since its goal is clear.

2. Behavior objectives help to *"set" listener expectations* when explained early in the presentation. When your audience knows they'll be doing something with your information (e.g. "At the end of my talk we'll each calculate our retirement benefits.") they are likely to pay closer attention and internalize the ideas presented.

3. Behavior objectives channel audience *participation which leads to greater understanding.* People can often talk about a concept without being able to apply it. Behavior objectives provide opportunities to try on new behaviors. *Doing* constitutes the only meaningful way in which learning takes place.

4. Behavior objectives can *inspire your listeners to apply* the new knowledge on their own. Once you've provided an opportunity to apply, you instill confidence in future application. The supervisor trainee who learns key features of the new union contract to the point that she can "repeat them back to you" (behavior objective) will feel much more confident explaining them to others.

5. Finally, behavior objectives permit an effective check-up phase to *evaluate your success in communicating.* There is no other way to determine if you're getting across than to observe some sort of behavior.

IF OBJECTIVES ARE SO GREAT, WHY DO SOME PEOPLE RESIST THEM?

Most speakers, even when they find it hard to say precisely what their objectives are, will concede that a presentation is an agent of change; as a result of listening, a person will somehow be different at the end from what he or she was at the beginning. Some speakers say that they cannot set objectives because the outcome of instruction may be different for every listener. If it is, I'd suggest your presentation has not been very successful.

The unexpressed difficulty—whether real or (more often) imagined—is that objectives are avoided because (1) the speaker isn't sure what he or she is trying to do, (2) the speaker sees the objectives as unmeasurable, or (3) the speaker is unaware of techniques for phrasing objectives in measurable ways. Further, as educator Peter Pipe explains:

> Measurable objectives—behavioral or performance objectives when we're talking about instruction—are easier to talk about than they are to do something about. Thanks in large part to the work of Robert F. Mager, many people are convinced that objectives are "a good idea." But lip service still outweighs application. And even among those who are working with objectives there are few who ask the larger question, "Where do these objectives come from?"[1]

Where *do* they come from? Let's look.

CREATING OBJECTIVES THAT WORK

Setting learning objectives means determining three things. First, we must identify specific behaviors we'd like to see in our listeners and describe the conditions under which these behaviors should occur. This becomes the minimum level of performance. Failing this, our talk could not be regarded as successful.

Secondly, we should determine when the observations will take place; set a timetable. Sometimes multiple observations are best; immediately following your message to check comprehension and later observations, perhaps on the job, to assess retention.

Finally, objectives should be quantifyable if at all possible. How often or how much of the new behavior should occur?

Let's look at some simple learning objectives one might set for an instructional presentation.

1. Immediately following the presentation, each listener will be able to calculate accurately his or her present retirement benefits.
   Specific behavior: accurately calculate earned benefits.
   Timetable: immediately following the presentation.

Quantity: his or her own.

2. Each listener will prepare and conduct three formal employee appraisals using management by objectives during the month of September.

Specific behavior: prepare and conduct employee appraisals using management by objectives approach.

Timetable: during September.

Quantity: three.

3. Each listener will identify and recycle all outdated forms to the Office Manager and replenish stock with current approved forms by October 1st.

Specific behavior: identify and recycle outdated forms to Office Manager; replenish with new forms.

Timetable: by October 1st.

Quantity: all.

Effective learning objectives depend upon a clear statement of *what* is to be done to demonstrate competence, *when* it is to be done, and *how much* or *how often*. Precise language is a key to developing such objectives.

STATING OBJECTIVES CLEARLY

In Chapter One I put forth some behavioral objectives for this book. Subsequent chapters each begin with a list of learning objectives. Take a look at the way these are worded. In each case, the objective expresses an action word which can be clearly visualized. Words like "explain," "describe," "name" and "apply" are preferred over words that express less observable responses like "understand" or "conceptualize."

Training specialist Robert F. Mager, whose name is widely associated with the concept of behavioral objectives, recommends using terms that are *concrete*—open to fewer interpretations—when phrasing objectives. He compares, for example these phrases:[2]

Words Open to Many Interpretations	*Words Open to Fewer Interpretations*
To know	to write
To understand	to recite
To *really* understand	to identify
To appreciate	to differentiate
To *fully* appreciate	to solve
To grasp the significance of	to construct
To enjoy	to list
To believe	to compare
To have faith in	to contrast

Use learning objectives to complete the sentence "When I've finished my presentation, my listeners should be able to . . ." Try this approach and add a crucial dimension to your informative presentation.

One final thought. In some business presentations it will not always be possible to test your success by actually having your listener recite or demonstrate something. Don't use that as an excuse for not using objectives. The behavioral objective's value is that it focuses your intent and permits the *possibility* of testing while the absence of such explicit goals does not.

ONE MORE TIME: GET YOUR LISTENERS INVOLVED

If you've read this book from front to back you're probably tired of hearing my next point. I promise to spare you one more flogging of the horse named Participation if you'll read just one short Chinese proverb.

I hear and I forget.
I see and I remember.
I do and I understand.

Communication is the creation of understanding. 'Nuff said.

LET YOUR LISTENERS KNOW YOU LIKE 'EM

Instructing others is a sharing of yourself. It is truly a noble venture. It's important that your listeners know that you sincerely want them to understand and to be able to apply what you show them. Instructional presentations are not the place for demonstrating what *you* know; that'll become self-evident as you help others.

Make it a point to convey a sense of concern for your listeners. One of the best principles of teaching I've ever heard can be apropos to any communication situation (and, I think, provides a good closing thought for this book on communication): "Nobody cares how much you know until they know how much you care."

INSTRUCTIONAL PRESENTATIONS: SPECIAL CONSIDERATIONS

Chapter 12. A summary of key ideas

1. Business presentations are functional communications. We must be concerned with whether or not they get the job done.

2. Predetermined learning objectives provide criteria against which we can measure the success of a presentation.
3. There are at least five advantages in using learning objectives:
    (a) They help the speaker keep an application focus.
    (b) They help "set" listener expectations.
    (c) They tie in with listener participation.
    (d) They inspire listeners to apply new information.
    (e) They permit evaluation of the speaker's success.
4. Speakers sometimes resist the use of measurable objectives because they
    (a) aren't sure exactly what they are trying to accomplish
    (b) see the goals of the talk as immeasurable
    (c) are unaware of techniques for phrasing objectives in measurable ways.
5. An effective learning objective will
    (a) clearly identify specific behavior targets
    (b) set a timetable for the occurrence of such behavior
    (c) describe how much of the behavior should occur.
6. In phrasing objectives, concrete, action-oriented terms which describe observable behaviors should be used.
7. Listener participation is crucial to the creation of understanding— especially in instructional presentations.
8. Convey a sense of concern for and genuine interest in your listeners. Avoid the temptation to show off what *you* know; that will become self-evident as you strive to help your listeners learn.

NOTES

1. Peter Pipe. *Objectives—Tools For Change* (Belmont, CA: Fearon, 1975), p. 3.
2. Robert F. Mager. *Preparing Instructional Objectives* (Belmont, CA: Fearon, 1962), p. 11.

APPENDIX

In this appendix you'll find extra copies of the following forms:

1. Conceptual planning: applying TIMM's CAT
2. Listener analysis checklist
3. Identifying central theme, key ideas and forms of support worksheet
4. Delivery critique form

These may be photocopied for use in developing your
FUNCTIONAL BUSINESS PRESENTATIONS

FIGURE 2-1
Conceptual planning: applying "TIMM'S CAT" to your presentation

1. TOPIC: Give your talk a label or a working title to help identify the message. Be sure your title indicates the importance of the topic to your audience.

2. INTENT: Specifically, what do you want your audience to learn, think, do, or feel? What are your learning objectives? Be realistic but do state your goals in some measurable way if possible. Include secondary reasons for giving the talk (create favorable image, etc.)

3. MATERIALS: How will you attempt to arrange the physical environment? What audio-visual aids will you use? Will you use notes or a manuscript to help you remember key points? What might be some creative alternatives to what you've been doing in the past?

4. MESSAGE: How will you get your listener's attention? What appeals will you use? How will you build the need development stage of your talk? How will you arrange the key ideas of your talk? What kind of action step will you use? Sketch out a brief outline.

5. SUMMARY: How will you use summaries to help your listeners remember your key points? Can certain ideas be clustered together? Can you use some sort of memory aids to help retention? (TIMM'S CAT is a memory aid).

6. CHECK-UP: Name several ways you can check up on what the audience has learned. Be creative and specific.

7. ASSIGNMENT: What kinds of assignments might be effective for your presentation? How can you get the audience to keep on thinking about your talk? How can you get them to try new behaviors?

8. TAKE-HOME: What items can you give your listeners that will keep on teaching after you've gone? How can you make these useful? How can you create a "family resemblance" among these items?

9. WHAT CAN YOU DO TO INCREASE LISTENER INVOLVEMENT IN WHAT YOU ARE SAYING? Specifically, how will you strive for more participation?

FIGURE 3-1
Listener analysis checklist

1. State your major purpose. What, precisely, do you want to happen in *this* audience as a result of your talk?

2. What specific advantages can you offer to this audience if they listen to you?

3. How much do they already know about your topic?

4. How resistant are they likely to be to your ideas? Why?

5. What kinds of evidence or information will likely be well received?

6. How can you find out more useful audience analysis information?

FIGURE 5-1
Identifying central theme, key ideas, and forms of support (worksheet)

1. Purpose: What are your objectives for this presentation? State them in terms of the *specific attitude change* or *course of action* you hope to bring about in the audience.

2. State your central theme clearly and concisely. (Be sure it meets the criteria suggested in this chapter.)

3. First list the key ideas you want your audience to understand. Next list the specific support information you will use for each key idea.
   Key Idea A
   Support Information

   Key Idea B
   Support Information

   Key Idea C
   Support Information

   Key Idea D
   Support Information

   Key Idea E
   Support Information

4. How will you attempt to project high credibility? Be specific.

FIGURE 10-1
Delivery critique form

Date: _____

Speaker: _____

Occasion: _____

1. Identify anything distracting in the opening moments of the talk. Check appearance, bearing, image projected, posture, positioning, and so forth.

2. How was the eye contact? Enough to create a strong sense of communication? Did the speaker look too much at some listeners and not enough at others?

3. How effective were the speaker's gestures, facial expressions, movement, and so forth? Identify anything distracting. Cite examples of good gestures.

4. Identify any mispronounced words or unclearly expressed terms.

5. How was the voice? Was the volume appropriate to the occasion? Was there sufficient variation in pitch, rate, timing, to hold listener interest? Was emphasis appropriate and helpful to understanding?

6. Identify any verbalized pauses or nonfluencies. (If this is a problem for the speaker, count the actual number of "um," "uh," "ah," "you know," expressed.)

INDEX

A

Abelson, Herbert I., 186
Allen, Fred, 118
Allen, Woody, 121
American Civil Liberties Union (ACLU), 76
Anatol, Karl W. E., 186
Anderson, Kenneth, 186
Applbaum, Ronald L., 186
Aristotle, 74, 82
Arrangement of ideas:
  cause-effect pattern, 91–92
  chronological pattern, 90
  criteria-application pattern, 90–91
  direct pattern, 87–88
  increasing magnitude or difficulty pattern, 94
  indirect pattern, 89–90
  order of importance pattern, 95
  problem-solution pattern, 93–94
Articulation, 157
Assignments given to listeners, 32–33
Assumptions, confusing with facts, 55–57
Attitude change, approaches to, 176–81
Attitudes, characteristics, 173–74
Audience, hostile, 45
Audience analysis. See Listener analysis.
Audience participation, 30, 34. See also Listener involvement.
Audience types, 42
Audio-visual aids, 28–29. See also Visual aids.
Auer, Jeffery, 7, 18

B

Behavioral science expectations, 15–16

Behavior change, approaches to, 176–81
Beisecker, Thomas D., 186
Bettinghaus, Erwin P., 186
Brembeck, Winston L., 186
Brooks, William D., 42, 48
Brown, James W., 150
Burgoon, Michael, 187
Business presentations versus public speaking, 13. See also Oral presentations.

C

Carlson, Conwell, 149
Central theme, 72–73
Chartmasters, Inc., 140–41
Check-up for listener comprehension, 31
Communication:
  barriers, 4–6, 17
  defined, 3, 6, 10
  efficiency versus effectiveness, 8–9, 17
  four basic skills, 7
  importance of skills, 2–3
  media choice, 8–9
  nonverbal, 32
Comparison or analogy as support for key ideas, 77
Conclusions, 112–13
Conditioning principle, 179–81
Consistency principle, 177–78
Coping quotient, 51–53
Corn, Ira G., 105, 114
Cox, Homer L., 18
Craig, Robert S., 130
Credibility:
  four primary dimensions, 75–76
  speaker ethos, 74
Cronkheit, Gary, 65, 70, 186